MOMENTS
IN OKLAHOMA
HISTORY

MOMENTS
IN OKLAHOMA
HISTORY
about people, places
things, and events

A BOOK OF TRIVIA

BY BONNIE SPEER

Also by Bonnie Speer:
Errat's Garden
Benjamin Stanley Revett:
   Father of Gold Dredging
Cleveland County, Pride of the Promised Land
The Great Abraham Lincoln Hijack
The Killing of Ned Christie, Cherokee Outlaw
Hillback To Boggy
Sons of Thunder
Write Your Life Story
Portrait of a Lawman, U.S. Deputy Marshal Heck Thomas
The Art of Self-Publishing

Library of Congress Catalog Card Number: 96-70454

ISBN 1-889683-01-9

Published by Reliance Press
1400 Melrose Drive
Norman, Oklahoma 73069

Printed in the United States of America

To Edna Mae Couch

TABLE OF CONTENTS

Introduction

INTRODUCTION

Oklahoma has a history like no other state. While most states were settled by the gradual westward movement of the pioneers, over one-half of Oklahoma was settled in chaotic land runs, and tent cities sprang into existence upon the prairies overnight.

Originally, Oklahoma had been set aside for removal of the Five Civilized Tribes in the East. During the Civil War, these tribes sided with the Confederacy. As a penalty, they were forced to surrender a portion of these lands for settlement of other tribes.

In 1879, word spread that 2,000,000 acres in the middle of Indian Territory were unassigned to any tribe. Agitation began among the "boomers" to open this land to homesteading. President Harrison signed the bill to do so on March 1, 1889. By proclamation, on March 23, he set the time for settlers to enter the lands at noon on April 22, 1889. It is estimated that over 100,000 settlers entered the land on opening day.

During the next 17 years, the remainder of Oklahoma Territory was opened to settlement through various land runs and by lottery. Boundary adjustments added to the state's size. At the time, Oklahoma Territory and Indian Territory existed side by side. Then in 1893, the Dawes Commission was appointed to negotiate with the Five Civilized Tribes to extinguish tribal titles to their lands. This work was completed in 1905, and with individual allotment of the land to tribal members, the way was paved for statehood. Oklahoma was admitted to the union as the 46th state on November 16, 1907.

Because of Oklahoma's unusual background, it has arrived at a level of progress within 100 years that has taken other areas hundreds of years to achieve. In the course of this development, many interesting characters have lived here, weaving their sagas into the colorful fabric of our heritage. That is what this book is all about, an overview of Oklahoma history, concerning the people, places, things, and events that make the state uniquely ours.

My research for this book came from numerous sources. I am sure I have missed many good stories, but my work was somewhat limited by the type of material I found at hand. Other times it was simply a matter of choice as I searched for items that could grab my attention, or could make me say, "I didn't know that!"

I wish to acknowledge a special thanks to Edna Mae Couch for the generous use of materials in her private collection. I don't know anyone better informed on the Oklahoma land runs than she. Without her assistance, my research would have been much more difficult. In addition, I would like to thank the staff at the Norman Public Library who were always ready to assist me in digging out little known facts, and to those individuals whom I have called on the phone or written to in verifying data. And last, I would like to thank my daughter, Cheryl Hanlon, for suggesting this project to me and encouraging me in it.

Bonnie Speer
Norman

PART 1. PRE-STATEHOOD

EARLY PEOPLE AND EXPLORERS
Seafarers may have visited Oklahoma
long before Columbus discovered America.

In 1961, University of Oklahoma archaeologists made a startling discovery in Caddo County, near Stecker. Buried beneath the deposits of the lower Domebo formation, they found the bones of a mammoth that had been killed by hunters. Several spear points still lay among the bones, and nearby, the workers found three more projectile points, two of which were identified as Clovis points. Subsequent radiocarbon testing dated these artifacts as being 11,200 years old. They are the earliest evidence of man in what is now Oklahoma.

Chinese monks may have explored central Oklahoma more than 3,000 years ago. During an archaeology excavation north of Luther in the late 1940s, workers found a finely carved statuette of wood that depicted the god of longevity, Shu Shing Lao, who was especially well known in China from 5 B.C. to 480 B.C. The statuette was carved from a tree known to be extinct for hundreds of years. It is believed that one of the early Chinese monks may have brought the statuette to Oklahoma, or that it was part of the loot from a robbery of that time.

Strangely enough, among the petroglyphs carved on the canyon walls of the Cimarron River in the Panhandle are symbols that were common throughout the ancient world. These symbols include sun symbols, the swastika, interlocked spirals and other designs. Some of these geometric symbols have even been found in New Zealand, Africa, Hawaii, Mexico, and South America. Where did the people come from who carved these symbols? No one knows but a legend among the Aztecs states that their ancestors came to North America from the lost continent of Atlantis.

Many people believe that the Phoenicians, Libyians, Iberic, Celtic, and Portuguese visited Oklahoma long before the time of Christ. Numerous images of ships have been found carved into stone in the valleys of the Arkansas, Canadian, and Cimarron rivers. The oldest carving, the Pontotoc Stone in Pontotoc County, is dated 500 B.C. Another major carving was discovered in the mesa country near the Oklahoma-Colorado border. Here on a cliffside is a forty-foot panel carved with strange ships and symbols from another century.

What happened to the residents of the Spiro Mounds in eastern Oklahoma is one of the great mysteries. From 750 A.D. to 1450 A.D., this site served as an important ceremonial center. Archaeological evidence shows it had a highly advanced culture with a sedentary way of life. Village craftsmen produced fine pottery, textiles, sculptures, and metal goods. They established extensive trade routes. Yet by 1450, for some unknown reason, those living here abandoned the site. Only a few priests remained to perform the sacred ceremonies. Soon these left too.

Some people believe the Vikings may have been among our state's earliest explorers. For years runeologists studied six strange markings carved on a slab of granite near Heavener. The markings were first discovered by the Choctaws in 1828. It was not until 1969 that a World War II cryptoanalysis expert deciphered the inscription: November 11,

1012. His news startled the world. The runestone indicated the Vikings had been here 400 years before the discovery of America by Columbus. Today, the inscription is preserved in the Runestone State Park.

In 1957, a road building crew was working on Highway 50, 11 miles north of Mooreland, when they noticed bits of wattle and a dozen flint chips in the earth. On investigation they found the outline of a log house, which had burned about 500 years before. A short distance away they found the remains of an even older house site, and from the trash pit they recovered pieces of charred human bones. Archaeologists concluded that these bones were the remains of a meal and that the residents of the two houses were possibly cannibals.

EUROPEAN DISCOVERY AND THE FIRST SETTLERS

Oklahoma was still an unknown wilderness during these days.

The Spanish were the first Europeans to cross Oklahoma and to keep a written record of their travels here. A large army marched across the plains of eastern New Mexico, the Staked Plains of Texas, and the Panhandle of Oklahoma into Kansas in search of Quivera, the fabled city of gold, during the 14th century. As they traveled across the Panhandle, the leader's name was left on Castle Rock, where the future Santa Fe Trail crossed the Cimarron River. Inscribed seventy years before the *Mayflower* landed at Plymouth Rock, it stated simply, "Coronatto, 1541."

According to local legend, Spanish gold seekers may have established a settlement in Devil's Canyon, south of Lugert, during the 16th century, from which they carried out extensive mining operations in the Wichita Mountains. The ruins of adobe houses, copper and iron implements, and other Spanish artifacts lend credence to the tale. The story is told that hostile Indians herded the Spaniards into a nearby canyon and killed them all. Many human bones have been found in the valley, and some say the area is haunted.

Ferdinandina was believed to be the first white settlement in present Oklahoma. Located six miles northeast of Newkirk, it was built on the site of a Caddoan village that dated back 700 centuries. Charles du Tisne, a French fur trader and trapper, first visited here in 1719. He erected a stockade of upright posts and established a trading post. As recently as 1870, British maps still showed the village as existing on the west bank of the Arkansas River, though it had disappeared long ago. The settlement was named after King Ferdinand VI of Spain.

Jean Pierre Choteau, a French fur trader, is often called the "Father of Oklahoma." Born in New Orleans, he was prominent in the early histories of St. Louis and Kansas City. In 1796, he headed west into an unknown region to establish a new trading post. He discovered an ideal spot on the Grand River. Here he founded the first permanent white settlement in what is now Oklahoma, at La Saline. In 1802, he induced 3,000 members of the Osage tribe to join him in the area, and with their trade, his business prospered.

INDIAN TERRITORY

Oklahoma was originally set aside for the Indians.

Nathaniel Pryor was the first person to volunteer his services to the Lewis and Clark expedition in 1802. After four years with the famous explorers, he spent an additional eight years in the army, and retired as a captain. Eventually he established a trading post near the mouth of the Verdigris River. Twice, Indians destroyed all he had. Sometimes he was called upon to act as councilor in negotiations with the Indians. Refused an old age pension, he died penniless in June 1831. Both a town and creek in Oklahoma bear his name, Pryor.

Early missionaries were astonished by the similarities between the religious tales of the Cherokees and biblical accounts. Among them the Indians related *Yehowa* was the name of a great being who had created the earth in seven days. When wickedness overcame the earth, *Yehowa* told a man to make a house that would swim, then take his family and different animals into it. After that it rained for 40 days and nights. These tales seemed so coincidental with those in the Bible it led some people to believe the Cherokees were the fabled lost tribe of Israel.

Sequoyah's elders laughed at him and his wife burned his work. A small, lame, mixed-blood, he got his first glimpse of "talking leaves" in 1813, while serving back East in a Cherokee regiment in the U.S. Army. When he went home, he began experimenting with making Cherokee sounds on paper. In 1821, after 12 years work, he produced a written language of 85 symbols, the first by an individual. When the syllabary was presented to the Cherokee National Council, within three days all could read and write. A salt maker, he later moved to Sallisaw.

Milly Frances is remembered as Oklahoma's own Pocahontas. During the first Seminole War in 1816, she begged two Indians to spare the life of a Georgia soldier, after the slaying of the two sisters by another white man. Finally the Indians agreed and sold the soldier into Spanish slavery instead. Years later he sought out Milly and offered to marry her, but she declined. In 1844, she was found living in a destitute condition in the Three Forks area. Congress granted her a $96 a month pension and a medal of honor for her heroism, but she died in 1847 before receiving either.

Fort Gibson was called the "Graveyard of the Army." It was the last frontier, the fartherest military outpost. It was established in 1824 to help keep peace among the Indians. But for many of the soldiers stationed here, it was literally a sentence of death, for the fort was located near the junction of the Arkansas and Neosho rivers. The land lay low and malaria and other diseases ran rampant here. Many died. Only the soldiers' nightly poker games and drunken celebrations relieved their boredom in this lonely outpost.

On May 15, 1832, the War Department issued regulations concerning the removal of Indians to Indian Territory. These stipulated no one could ride in a wagon, nor on horseback, during the 1,200 mile journey except the infirm or very young.

They could take nothing except necessary clothing, bedding, light cookware, and a few agriculture and mechanical tools. Only one wagon was allowed for baggage transportation for every 150 persons. One-fourth of the Indians died on this journey, making the "Trail of Tears" the saddest story in our nation's history.

General Sam Houston was the first practicing lawyer in what is today Oklahoma. A former governor of Tennessee and a national hero, he had fled from a broken marriage to join his Cherokee friends in Indian Territory. He established a trading post on the Neosho River, and during his three and a half years there, he helped the Cherokees expand their legal system. Described as a brilliant courtroom lawyer, with a gift as a "talker," he went on to become the hero of Texas in its fight for independence from Mexico.

In the officers' circle in Fort Gibson National Cemetery, lies the grave of Sam Houston's Cherokee wife, Tiana Rogers. Nearby is the grave of another woman, marked only as "Vivia." Legend says she was a teenage girl in love with a soldier, who followed him to his post at Fort Gibson, where she masqueraded as a young lieutenant. Here she took sick and died. Her true sex was discovered after her death. In a quandary, Fort Gibson officials asked Washington headquarters what they should do in regard to her body. The reply was, "Bury, and say nothing."

Cynthia Ann Parker was captured by Comanches during a raid on Fort Parker, near Groesbeck, Texas, in 1836, at the age of nine. She grew up among the Comanches and married a war chief, Peta Noconi, and had three children. Her son, Quannah, was a young boy when she and her daughter, Prairie Flower, were recaptured by Texas Rangers and returned to Texas in 1860. Four years later, both mother and daughter were dead.

Legend says Cynthia tried many times to return to her Comanche family and that she died of a broken heart.

On November 28, 1864, Chief Black Kettle's Cheyenne village was attacked and massacred by Colorado troops at Sand Creek. Black Kettle realized the Indians would have to make peace with the white men or be annihilated. He signed the Peace Treaty at Medicine Lodge in 1867, and accepted a reservation for his trouble. However, the government failed in its promises and warfare broke out again. This led to the Battle of Washita on November 27, 1868, almost four years to the day after the first massacre, and ironically, the Peace Chief and his wife were the first to die.

In 1865, Army scout Kit Carson made a big mistake. The War Department ordered him to locate a fort in New Mexico near the 103rd Meridian for the protection of travelers on the Santa Fe Trail. Carson selected a site on a high knoll, on the banks of Carrizo Creek. Here he established the fort, bringing rocks from the creekbed for the walls, barracks and headquarters. A sentry tower commanded a sweeping view of the plains and Santa Fe Trail. All of which was fine except for one thing: he had located Fort Nichols four miles east of the New Mexico boundary — in Oklahoma.

Fort Sill was established on December 29, 1868, when a troop under Colonel Grierson arrived at Medicine Bluff. Located on the site of an old Wichita Indian village, it was originally called Camp Wichita. Headquarters moved from Fort Gibson to Camp Wichita in March along with the regiment of the Tenth Cavalry. The Buffalo Soldiers began construction on the post immediately. The soldiers served as "an army of occupation" among the Kiowas, Comanches, Southern Cheyennes, and Arapahoes as these tribes settled down to reservation life.

The Cherokee gobble was an unearthly sound, between the howl of a coyote and the gobble of a turkey. The Indians uttered it in defiance against an opponent, and when setting out on expeditions. The fullbloods in the Union Army produced such a great cry in battle, that the noise frightened the enemy. Once a defendant in the Fort Smith court testified he had killed another because the man had gobbled at him. The court was astounded at the flippancy of the excuse until it was explained the cry meant sudden death to all in his path.

In 1874, the government was trying to decide where to establish the Union Agency for the Five Civilized Tribes. Eufaula was giving Muskogee a pretty strong tussle for the honor. So Washington officials sent an inspector to Indian Territory to determine which town could best take care of its employees. On the night before his arrival, a resident of Muskogee dumped a barrel of salt into Eufaula's town well; after one taste of the water, the inspector said agency headquarters would be located in Muskogee.

Amos Chapman, the chief of scouts at Camp Supply, was a one-legged man. He had left home when 16 and wandered onto the Cheyenne Reservation where he became a trader and scout. On September 12, 1874, he was serving under General Nelson A. Miles when his ankle was shattered during a fight with Kiowas at the Battle of Buffalo Wallow. After the five survivors were rescued three days later, his leg was amputated below the knee. He received the Congressional Medal of Honor for his valor in the fight, and continued to serve as chief of scouts until 1891.

On July 4, 1874, Pat Hennessy, an Indian Territory freighter, and three of his drivers were massacred during the last of the Indian uprisings. Hennessy was found tied to a wheel in the burning remains of his wagon on the Chisholm Trail. After the grisly discovery, the bodies of the men were buried nearby. Some blamed the killings on hostile Cheyenne and Osage Indians, but others believed the atrocity had been committed by white outlaws. A town was named in Hennessy's honor, but unfortunately it was misspelled, Hennessey.

Jake Bartles proved a sore loser. The first white man to live in the Coo-wees-coo-wee district of the Cherokee Nation, he established a grist mill and the first electricity plant on the north bank of the Caney River in 1875, and built the first store here. Then two of his clerks quit and went into competition across the river. Their side of the town grew faster. When it incorporated, the two men named the town Bartlesville in Bartles' honor, but he wanted no part of it and moved his home and store four miles away where he started the town of Dewey.

Jim Quinlan was a quiet, soft-spoken man who worked as a government teamster at Fort Supply for $35 a month and rations. He saved his money until he had enough to operate a Mexican monte bank at the isolated settlement. He ran an honest game, and never played a hand himself. People came from miles around to participate in the game. Within a few years, he collected $60,000 from his percentages. He took a trip back East and bought a fine farm for his parents, then he returned to Fort Supply to die on July 12, 1877, at the age of 32 with tuberculosis.

Amos Chapman, the famous one-legged chief of scouts at Camp Supply, served there for 17 years. Once he attended a Cheyenne pow-wow where the presence of a white man was not appreciated. Unpreturbed, he approached the kettle of dog soup the Cheyennes were making, thrust his right leg into the boiling pot, and stirred vigorously, his clothing concealing his artificial limb. The Indians stared, startled. Chapman withdrew his leg then sat down in the circle of the bravest warriors, where he was readily accepted. "Big medicine, no burn leg," they said.

Chief Joseph and the Nez Percés were brought to Indian Territory as prisoners from their home in Idaho in late 1877, following an extraordinary Indian war. Throughout, they had displayed a courage and skill that won universal praise. They abstained from atrocities on peaceful families, and fought with scientific skill while being chased towards Canada. Finally on October 5, they were forced to surrender and exiled from their beloved land. Placed on a reservation just west of present Tonkawa, here they remained until 1885, always longing to return home.

Geronimo was the feared leader of the Chiricahua Apaches, and the most cunning of all Indians. His warriors were said to have killed 2,500 people in Arizona alone. He and his tribe surrendered to army troops on September 4, 1886. As prisoners of war, they were sent first to Florida, then Alabama, after which they were transferred to Fort Sill in October 1894. Here they lived peaceably in scattered villages and adapted easily to farming. Geronimo became a celebrity, traveling with Pawnee Bill's Wild West Circus, and even dictated his biography.

In 1888, word came from Wovoka, a Paiute Indian in Nevada, that God was coming soon to right the wrongs done to His Red Children. The message spread like wildfire in Indian Territory. Wovoka instructed all in a special dance and said the Indians must keep peace with the white man. The Indians looked forward to the coming of the Messiah. But on the appointed day nothing happened, and many lost faith. Even so, Wovoka's message proved helpful as the Plains tribes adjusted to a new life and adopted the peaceful philosophy of the Ghost Dance.

Civilizing the Indians placed on reservations in Oklahoma proved ro easy task. In 1893, the U.S. government set about teaching the Kickapoos at Shawnee how to farm. Agents distributed free wagons, horses, and farm machinery. They built new frame homes for the Kickapoos. However, it wasn't long before they discovered the Indians had cut large holes in the roofs of their new homes. On investigation, officials found the Indians had sold their stoves, chopped up the wooden floors for firewood, and built their fires on the earthen floors.

It was a poignant moment. Prior to 1900, thousands of buffalo had roamed the Oklahoma prairies, and nomadic Indians had followed them. Then came the buffalo hunters with their big guns and blasted the animals into near extinction. Far-sighted friends acted to save the buffalo. On October 11, 1907, six bulls and nine cows arrived on the train at Cache from the New York Zoological Park. On hand to greet them were the last Comanche chief, Quannah Parker, scores of his people and Kiowa tribal elders. All had tears in their eyes at seeing something they thought long gone.

Alice Brown Davis was the first woman to become chief of one of the Five Civilized Tribes. The daughter of a Scotsman and a full-blood Seminole woman, she was born in the Cherokee Nation at Park Hill in 1852. Moving to the Seminole Nation after her marriage, she remained active in tribal business throughout her adult life. Her older brother served as chief of the Seminole Nation for thirty years. In 1922, President Warren G. Harding appointed Alice to succeed her brother. She continued to serve as Chief of the Seminoles for 13 years.

EARLY CATTLE INDUSTRY

Following the Civil War,
many cattle trails and ranches
developed in Indian Territory.

Montford T. Johnson was known as the "Chickasaw Rancher." In 1865, he became interested in establishing a ranch near present day Purcell. Jesse Chisholm warned him that the Kiowas and Comanches would tolerate his presence only as long as he refrained from using white cowboys. Texans in particular were resented by these tribes. The rancher heeded his friend's advice and employed only Negroes, Indians, and Mexicans to patrol his range. Pioneering in importing Durham bulls to upgrade his stock, his ranch become one of the largest in the area.

From 1867 to 1880, 14 million head of cattle were driven through Indian Territory from Texas to the cattle markets in Kansas. The most popular trail was the Chisholm Trail, which passed just west of Oklahoma City. Ironically, Jesse Chisholm, the man who loaned his name to the trail, never saw it used as a cattle trail. He had established several trading posts on his supply route from the Arkansas River near Wichita to the North Canadian River near present day Yukon. Because he marked that portion of the trail, (which was in reality the old Wichita trace), his name was applied to its entire length.

The early Oklahoma cowboy was an international product. He adopted most of his equipment and clothing from Mexico, which in turn had borrowed them from Spain. Each piece was functional. The wide sombrero provided shade, and the bat-winged chaparejos protected his legs from the thick brush. His neckerchief kept the dust out of his lungs. His lasso and the method of roping on horseback were also adopted from the Spanish as were his "piggin' string" and the custom of branding livestock, which the Spanish had borrowed from the Moors of Castile.

The Cheyenne and Arapahoe Cattle Company was the largest ranch in Indian Territory. Better known as the C & A, it was organized in 1878 to lease the Cheyenne and Arapahoe Reservation grasslands. Covering a million acres, its boundary ran from the Cherokee Strip south to the Washita River, and from the West Texas border east to the Dodge City Cattle Trail. Some of the Indians protested the lease, and a constant state of war existed with the cowboys. Finally, President Cleveland ordered all cattle off the reservation by July 25, 1885.

At the peak of its existence, the 101 Ranch covered parts of four Oklahoma counties and encompassed three towns. It employed hundreds of people who produced and manufactured everything they needed. The ranch did not derive its name from its size as many think but from a barroom fight in Texas. During an early cattle drive, the owner had let his cowboys visit San Antonio one night, where they wrecked a saloon. To remind them of their misdeed, he branded the saloon's name, 101, on the cattle, so that the cowboys had to stare at it the next two months as they trailed the herd northward.

PART 2. SETTLING THE LAND

THE OKLAHOMA LAND RUN

Oklahoma had a beginning like no other state.

In 1879, in a passion of revenge, Elias C. Boudinot published an article in the *Chicago Tribune* which triggered the Boomer movement and the subsequent Oklahoma Land Run. He stated that 2,000,000 acres in the heart of Indian Territory were unassigned to any tribe and was therefore public domain and subject to homestead. A half-blood Cherokee, his intent was to destroy the Cherokee Nation. Tribal leaders had murdered his father in 1839 for ceding Eastern Cherokee lands to the federal government for Western lands. Boudinot never forgave them.

David L. Payne was hailed as "Prince of the Boomers." After three years with the Fourth Kansas Infantry during the Civil War, he was elected to the Kansas Legislature in 1864. Rejoining the army, he was at Appomattox Court House when General Robert E. Lee surrendered. He served as captain in the Nineteenth Kansas Cavalry with Custer during most of his Washita campaign. A doorkeeper in the National House of

Representatives for four years, he became the leader of the Boomer invasion into Oklahoma, but he died before his dreams could materialize.

William Couch was one of David Payne's most trusted lieutenants. He took over as leader of the Boomers following Payne's untimely death in 1884. On opening day of the Unassigned Lands, he staked a claim to 160 acres west of Oklahoma City. He was elected the city's first mayor and served for seven months. On April 14, 1890, he was wounded in a gunfight over his claim. He died 17 days later, almost one year to the day of the opening. Like Payne, he had given his best to the settlement of Oklahoma but did not live to enjoy the fruits of his efforts.

Pawnee Bill was better known for his wild west show than his Boomer activities, but at the time he seemed right for the job. He was a showman, pioneer, and a national figure who maintained the respect of the people. It was the idea of the Wichita Board of Trade to send for him. Things had stalled in Congress and it seemed the Oklahoma lands would never be settled. Pawnee Bill organized a Boomer colony, and planned to force the opening. He moved his colony to Arkansas City on January 28, 1889, then word came that Congress had passed the Oklahoma bill.

Oklahoma Bugher was the first white child to be born in what is present Oklahoma. On the day of her birth, April 10, 1889, her parents, Mr. and Mrs. Lewis Bugher, were camped in a tent on the Santa Fe right-of-way in what is now Oklahoma City, and she was named by the soldiers guarding the territory. After her birth, her parents moved across the Canadian River to await the opening of the Unassigned Lands at Purcell. Bugher homesteaded on 160 acres northeast of Lexington in Cleveland County. The first territorial census incorrectly listed Oklahoma as a boy.

Arkansas City, Kansas, was the major gathering point for those making the run on April 22, 1889. Fully 10,000 persons clamored to board the first of fifteen trains that left at 11 a.m. to cross the Cherokee Strip to the border of the Unassigned Lands. When the signal was given at noon, with a shriek of the whistle, the trains joined the mad race for land. The excitement on the trains rose to an unbelievable pitch with everyone hollering and waving handkerchiefs and flags. Some people tumbled off the trains to claim quarter-section homesteads, but the majority took town lots in Guthrie and Oklahoma City.

On April 22, 1889, when the Unassigned Lands were settled, two companies established townsites at Oklahoma Station and immediately began surveying streets. Conflict arose at once and a Committee of Fourteen was elected to settle the land dispute. The committee began resurveying at the southern edge of South Oklahoma City, but when it reached Grand Avenue, it found that if that area were to be resurveyed many of the original claimants would lose their lots. So they compromised, and the result is the sudden jog in today's Sheridan (Grand) Avenue.

The first Oklahomans were choosy folks. In the chaos which followed the settlement of Oklahoma City, a mass meeting was called on the second day to elect a committee to resurvey the townsite. Voters rejected General James Baird Weaver, a veteran congressman from Iowa, who had been instrumental in opening the Oklahoma lands. He had been the Greenback Party's presidential candidate in 1880. Three years later, after being rejected for the survey committee, Weaver polled more than a million votes as the People's Party presidential candidate.

During the Run of 1889, any man or single woman 21 years of age or older could stake a 160-acre claim, but had to live on it at least six months of the year. Chickasaw resident R. M.

Graham, his two sons, and a hired man laid claim to an entire section of land near Lexington. Four months later when Graham's daughter turned 21, the hired man relinquished his claim to her. Graham then built a house at the point where the four claims came together. Each claimant had a bedroom on his or her own land, thus fulfilling the letter of the law.

The intrepid Nanitta Daisey made three runs into Oklahoma. The first was on April 22, 1889, when she leaped from the cowcatcher of a slow moving train to stake her claim two miles north of Edmond. Next she entered the Fox and Sac land rush on September 22, 1891, but her horse fell and she was knocked unconscious. She made a third run into the Cherokee Strip in 1893 and became involved in a dispute over a Perry townsite. She was a former schoolteacher and correspondent for the *Fort Worth Gazette*, *Dallas Morning News*, and *Louisville Courier-Journal.*

TERRITORIAL LIFE

Oklahoma was the land of opportunity for many.

Among the most ambitious men who settled in Guthrie on April 22, 1889, were three who decided to open a bank. They counted their assets that first night and found they had a total of $8.31 among them. Undaunted, they secured some blank promissory notes, each signed one for $10,000, and they exchanged them. Next morning, they opened their bank with advertised assets of $30,000. Business was good from the beginning. They kept the money in a pot-bellied stove until they could obtain a better vault, the founders of Guthrie's first bank.

"Button Mary" became a familiar figure in Guthrie after the run. She arrived on the day of the opening and set up her tent beside the railroad track. One of the town's more enterprising citizens, each morning at sunrise, she left her camp and made her rounds through the busy tent city with needle and thread in hand. Each time she met a man with a missing button on his clothing, she sewed one on then requested a dime for her work. If he paid her, all was well and good, but if he didn't he received a sharp jab with the needle.

Henry Ives, who came to Guthrie on the day of the Run of 1889, was shocked at the lack of sanitary conditions in the new tent town. Deciding to do something about it, he dug a deep hole on his lot, then securing a quantity of leafy limbs from Cottonwood Creek, he planted them upright around the hole, and erected a sign: "Rest Room, 10 cents." Business was good, but rivals eventually forced him to lower his prices to five cents. Even so, when his enterprise was no longer needed, he had earned enough money to open a harness repair shop.

No one knows why Joseph Foucart left Europe. Once the king of Belgium's private architect, he arrived in Guthrie in June 1889. There he found an architect's dream, a city to be built. Within eight months he had designed and built six magnificent buildings. All reflected his European background. Looking like castles, palaces, and fortresses, they made Guthrie the showplace of the Southwest. He designed Northwestern State's administration building and OSU's Williams Hall, then he disappeared again as mysteriously as he had arrived, Oklahoma's first architect.

They called 1890 the "Year of the Turnips." The settlers had arrived too late to plant a crop that spring of 1889, and by June drought had set in. Claims were abandoned by the score. Railroad companies sold seed to the settlers on credit. That fall when it rained, almost every available acre was planted in turnips, about the only thing that would grow that late in the season. This produced tons of turnips, for man and his animals. The starving homesteaders were able to survive during 1890 on the turnips, but it was an experience none cared to repeat.

That first year following the Run of 1889 was a severe one for many of the homesteaders. Many had arrived with little to their name, and it was too late in the year to plant much. Some were on the verge of starvation by the time spring came. The government set up a Board of Relief in the fall of 1890. Here destitute families could receive 25 pounds of flour, and five pounds each of bacon, beans, and salt. Many wept at the disgrace of being considered a pauper, but swallowed their fierce pride and accepted the meager handouts.

In December 1890, a group of businessmen formed a plan to dig a canal on the west side of Oklahoma City to furnish electrical power for the downtown area. The canal would be six miles long with a fall of 32.6 feet. That winter hundreds of men worked on the project and thousands of dollars were poured into it. A new grist mill and generating plant were built. When the North Canadian River was turned into the canal, the project looked successful, but within three days the water was all gone, absorbed by the sandy soil. So the Grand Canal was abandoned.

In December 1890, a near penniless carpenter drifted into Norman, looking for work. A local businessman hired him to help erect a two-story rock building on West Main Street for $1.50 a day. Later this building was to house the first classes for the University of Oklahoma. The carpenter, unable to find more work in Norman, went on to Colorado where, on July 4, 1891, he staked a claim at Cripple Creek, which he called the "Independence." Two years later, he struck it rich. His name was Winfield Scott Stratton.

Mail order brides were not unusual in Oklahoma following the land runs. In 1892 a group of Norman citizens banded together to supply the local demand. Called the Widowers Mutual Protective Association, its stated intent was to "encourage matrimonial alliance with all widowers and widows of Norman." The association promised to furnish entertainment for the wedding feast, a covered wagon, stove, and provisions for at least 20 days for a honeymoon trip. The association fell apart when James Bishop, one of the organizers, got married.

A stout, dowdy woman with an indomitable will and a hatred of liquor settled near Seiling in 1892 with her minister husband. The next 15 years she roamed Oklahoma and Kansas denouncing the evils of alcohol and smashing saloons with her trusty hatchet. Her campaign in Oklahoma, and that of other members of the Women's Christian Temperance Union, paid off, for at statehood the citizens voted for prohibition. It would be another 50 years before a legal drink could be obtained in the state again, thanks to the temperance agitator, Carry Nation.

Of the 57 students who enrolled in the first classes at the University of Oklahoma, on September 15, 1892, not one of them qualified for freshman standing. Since the opening of the Unassigned Lands, few high schools had been established in the new territory, and those that did exist had not had time to graduate any students. So that entire first class at OU was admitted to preparatory courses, completing their high school requirements, and it was not until 1893 that the first college student was enrolled in the university.

Woodward's first madam, Mary Eliza "Miss Dolly" Kizer, arrived in 1893. She had worked some of the best brothels in Denver during the silver boom of the late 1800s. She managed the other "working girls" at the Dew Drop Saloon until one day in May 1899, after an all night party at the annual Livestock Association convention, she realized she and her girls looked cheap, even in their finest. She decided to leave the redlight district, filed on a homestead claim, sold her jewelry, and paid the way home for all of her girls who wished to go.

OTHER LAND OPENINGS

On May 2, 1890, Congress passed the Organic Act, creating the Territory of Oklahoma.

Most areas in Oklahoma Territory experienced the excitement of a land run only once. However, this place went through the fun twice. On April 22, 1889, 50,000 people gathered here to race south into the Unassigned Lands which was opened by proclamation by President Benjamin Harrison. On September 15, 1893, thousands more gathered at the same place to race north into the Cherokee Outlet, opened by proclamation of President Grover Cleveland. It was the east-west boundary line between the two areas, located three miles north of Stillwater.

While other towns in Oklahoma Territory burst into being during one of the general land runs, this one staged its own private land run. What is today Lincoln County once belonged to the Kickapoo, Sac and Fox, and Iowa Indians. The area was opened to settlement on September 22, 1891. But on the day of that run, this town was not ready. Government surveyors were running late. So the 320-acre townsite was set aside until they could finish their work. On September 28, 1891, 5,000 settlers rushed in to claim the 94 blocks of Chandler.

It was a most ambitious land grab. Before the opening of the Cherokee Outlet in 1893, a pair of enterprising brothers ran cattle north of what is now Mooreland in northwestern Oklahoma. The two ranchers hired 150 extra hands to make the run and to stake a claim. On each claim these cowboys erected a four-foot square "house," then relinquished the claim to the brothers. After all, nowhere in the rules for the run did the government state the size of the needed improvement. A town was later established and named in honor of the Quinlan brothers.

The most famous picture of the Oklahoma land runs was taken at the opening of the Cherokee Strip on September 19, 1893. William Prettyman is credited with the photo but the name of the real photographer remains a mystery. Prettyman, an Arkansas City photographer, had built an observation tower on the boundary line. There he posted three photographers to capture the start of the race. One of the plates was so clear that it became the most requested picture in the world. Prettyman never revealed which of the three photographers had snapped the picture.

In 1893, Bethsheba, an all-female town with a population of 33, was established between Perry and Enid. A local editor sent a reporter to get the story. The mayor held him off with a shotgun. From neighbors he learned that even all the animals in the town were female. The mayor was from Kansas and had been married to a traveling salesman until she found he was already married and had five children. Trouble erupted in

Bethsheba though when the women found they couldn't physically handle some tasks. Twelve women deserted the town after the first week. One night the remainder folded their tents and disappeared.

On August 6, 1901, the federal government settled the Kiowa-Comanche and Apache reservations by lottery instead of a chaotic land run as in the other Oklahoma land openings. Registration points were established at El Reno and Lawton. Here more than 165,000 persons registered for the 13,000 claims. Following the drawing for the claims, all winners in the lottery were notified, but 1,362 homesteaders failed to appear at the land office on the proper day to claim their homestead, and the land reverted to the government.

In 1901, Fort Sill was already established, so when the townsite for Lawton was laid out, it was bounded on three sides by federal land or school land. Therefore, there was little chance for a homesteader to obtain a valuable claim adjoining the townsite. The southern one-mile boundary allowed for only two 160-acre claims. J. F. Woods, who drew first selection in the land lottery, chose his 160-acres in a long strip along the entire boundary, forcing the second claimant, Mattie Beal, to choose a strip farther back. This action earned him the nickname of "Hog" Woods, and so he is still known by that name today.

Mattie Beal was the sweetheart of the Oklahoma Land Lottery. When the federal government opened the Kiowa-Comanche reservation for settlement in 1901, her name was the second one drawn in the lottery to select a 160-acre claim. A 22-year-old Wichita telephone operator, she instantly became rich and a celebrity. She received over 500 proposals of marriage by mail, none of which she answered. When she married a year later, she and her husband built an elegant home and she became one of Lawton's most gracious hostesses.

PART 3. DEVELOPING THE LAND

STATEHOOD

*Oklahoma's politics were forged
in the heat of battle.*

Kate Barnard was one of the first women in America elected to public office. During the Oklahoma Constitutional Convention, which convened on November 20, 1906, she crusaded for legal reform. She wrote the Democrat platform measures in regard to children, the poor, and the imprisoned. She worked so hard and skillfully during the convention that the office of Commissioner of Charities and Corrections was written into the constitution for her. During the first statehood election, she received more popular votes than Governor Haskell. She served two four-year terms.

They called it the "Squirrel Rifle Brigade." It was formed in jest to protect the original parchment of the Oklahoma State Constitution. Following the constitutional convention in 1907, chairman Bill Murray had refused to turn the document over to the Secretary of State. Instead he carried it home with him in a strong box. The public raised a furor over the "sight unseen" constitution. Years later Murray explained his action. He had caught a copyist making changes in the controversial corporations article and after that he trusted no one with the document.

When Oklahoma became a state on November 16, 1907, 556 saloons were forced to close. That final day was an orgy in many towns. Men who had never been known to drink before, became drunk, and the old boozers fought it harder than ever. Small boys caught the fever, and securing liquor in some manner, became staggering drunk. At some saloons a fight raged all day and into the night. Finally at 11:50 p.m., all the drunks were dragged into the streets, the lights were extinguished, and the doors were locked. Prohibition had arrived.

After a 20-year fight, Oklahoma City obtained the state capital from Guthrie on June 11, 1910. The move was expected to be made in 1913. However, that night Governor Charles Haskell ordered the official state seal secretly removed to Oklahoma City. There at 6 a.m., on Lee-Huckins Hotel letterhead, he proclaimed Oklahoma City the capital. Later he said he had done so because he was tired of Frank Greer, the viperative editor of the *Oklahoma State Capital*, calling him a liar every morning. Ironically, Greer's paper folded one year from that day.

Oklahoma had no state prison, so officials contracted with Kansas to keep their convicts. A growing number of complaints led Kate Barnard, Commissioner of Charities and Corrections, to investigate Lansing prison. There she found Oklahoma prisoners working in coal mines under deplorable conditions, and being punished in inhumane "water holes." As a result legislators hastened the building of the McAlester state penitentiary, and passed laws preventing the abuse of prisoners, and use of convict contract labor, laws which still stand today.

Called the "Sage of Tishomingo," William H. Murray had a greater influence on Oklahoma than any other politician. He was leader of the Sequoyah convention, president of Oklahoma's Constitutional Convention, first speaker of the House, and a member of Congress. He marshaled the dry forces at statehood, and while governor during the Great Depression, he called out the national guard 34 times. In 1932, he was a candidate for president of the United States. Nicknamed "Alfalfa Bill" because of his exhortations to grow the legume, he died destitute in 1956.

Dry Oklahoma legalized beer again on July 12, 1933. Enterprising businessmen organized a "Run of 1933" to supply thirsty Oklahomans. Five railroad trains loaded with the coveted beverage were soon under steam at key border points, ready to dash across the state line as soon as the state attorney general announced that beer was legal. However, Governor "Alfalfa Bill" Murray had other ideas. He called out the National Guard to stop the trains. He said the state had spent 26 years bone-dry and could remain so a little longer.

Oklahoma has impeached twice as many governors as any other state. Governor John Walton was removed from office in 1923 on charges of misuse of his power of pardon and parole, suspension of the writ of habeas corpus, and repeated declarations of martial law. Governor Henry S. Johnston was impeached by the twelfth legislature on January 21, 1929, for incompetency. Governor David Hall barely missed impeachment and was arrested shortly after the completion of his term in 1975, on charges of kickbacks in office and was subsequently sentenced to prison.

It was a rare occurrence. On January 12, 1931, 12,000 people gathered at the capital steps in Oklahoma City for the inauguration of "Alfalfa Bill" Murray. They watched as he was sworn in as Oklahoma's ninth governor by his 91-year-old father, Uriah Dow Murray, acting in his capacity as notary public. Twenty-eight years later, in 1950, William Murray had the pleasure of swearing in his own son, Johnston T. Murray, as governor, thus they became Oklahoma's only father-son duo to serve as head of state.

At one time Oklahoma had a law providing for nine-foot-long sheets on hotel and sleeping car beds. The bill came about because of the poor accommodations the incumbent governor found as he traveled about the state. The bill made him the laughing stock of his political opponents, but the average citizen appreciated his thought. For it was believed that a sheet long enough to fold back over the seldom washed blankets was the traveling man's best protection against disease. Sponsored by Governor William Murray, it was the Murray-Whitehead bill.

During the Depression, Oklahoma had little money for highways. Expensive bridges were often built by private toll bridge companies. Then in 1930, Oklahoma built a free bridge across the Red River. A Denison, Texas, toll bridge company filed suit in Federal court stating Oklahoma's free bridge would destroy its trade. The judge issued an injunction forbidding the opening of the free bridge. But Governor Murray ordered the National Guard to close the Oklahoma end of the toll bridge, and with nowhere to go, the bridge company was forced to quit.

LAW AND ORDER

Oklahoma was a notorious land for many years.

The Light Horsemen of the Choctaws were all that their name implied, a hard-fighting, straight-shooting body of men who carried no excess equipment. Their horse, saddle, revolver, and rifle were their only standard gear, and their rations consisted of a few handsful of parched corn and jerked beef. Moving swiftly from place to place, sometimes they joined forces with United States deputy marshals in an attempt to rid Indian Territory of the renegades and other tough characters who infested the region in the 1880s.

Ezekiel Proctor was one of the few individuals with whom the United States ever made a peace treaty. A half-breed Cherokee, he was accused of murdering a white woman in 1872. Charged in Indian court, during the trial at Whitmire schoolhouse, a federal posse arrived, claiming jurisdiction. Gunfire erupted and 11 men died. The government accused the prisoner and his followers of the deaths and they fled. The Cherokee Nation threatened to revolt over the right to control its own courts. Finally, on August 13, 1873, President Grant granted Proctor a treaty of amnesty.

Judge Issac Parker exerted more influence in Indian Territory than any other man. He came to Fort Smith in 1875 to take over as head of the federal court of the Western District of Arkansas, which included present Oklahoma. During his 21-year reign, he docketed more than 13,000 cases and imposed sentences on some 9,000 offenders. He sentenced 160 men to the gallows, and hanged 79. For this he was nicknamed the "Hanging Judge." Congress stripped him of his jurisdiction in 1896. Two and a half months later, Parker died, some said of a broken heart.

Heck Thomas was considered the best deputy marshal to ever operate out of the Fort Smith federal court. He served in the Civil War at the age of 12, and later helped capture the Sam Bass gang in Texas. At Fort Smith he always brought in the largest number of prisoners from Indian Territory. On November 21, 1887, he scored a record with 47 prisoners, who had traveled in seven wagons a distance of 275 miles. He gained fame in Oklahoma Territory as one of "The Three Guardsmen," and served as first police chief of Lawton.

In 1887, a 30-man posse turned a cannon upon a desperate outlaw, the only such instance in history. The outlaw, a former member of the Cherokee Executive Committee, had been accused of murdering a United States deputy marshal in Tahlequah. For five years the outlaw eluded law officers in the Cherokee hills, defending himself in a log fortress. Finally a posse blasted him out with the cannon and dynamite, killing him as he attempted to escape. Thirty years later an eyewitness to the murder of the deputy marshal exonerated the outlaw, Ned Christie.

Belle Starr gained fame as the Bandit Queen, yet there is no record that she ever killed anybody, engaged in confidence games, or directed a band of outlaws. Born Myra Belle Shirley in 1848, she had a violent temper, consorted with men outside the law, carried a pistol, and went to prison for horse theft in 1885. Early in 1889 she was blasted off her horse and killed by an unknown assailant in a cornfield near her home in Indian

Territory. Writers quickly picked up her story and enhanced it, making her famous as the outlaw queen.

It was against the law in the Choctaw Nation to sell or to manufacture "Choc" beer. But those in the European mining communities of McAlester and Krebs ignored this. Many housewives brewed the drink, and the miners insisted it was essential to their health because of the bad water in their area, though that in adjacent neighborhoods strangely proved good. They swore they used the beer as a tonic rather than a beverage, and physicians abetted them. Made of barley, hops, tobacco, fishberries, and a small amount of alcohol, "Choc" beer supported a way life.

During its first 20 years, Oklahoma City politics were ruled by "Big Anne," Queen of the Redlight District. Anne Wynn had pitched her tent across the street from the Santa Fe Depot on the day of the run. A shrewd, intelligent, fashionable looking woman, it was said most of the city officials and some of the policemen were on her payroll. She built one of the plushiest bawdy houses west of the Mississippi, and reportedly, more deals were made here than in City Hall. Acquitted of murder in 1908, she moved to California, thus ending her reign.

In summer of 1889, a drunk with a gun kept interrupting a group of men on the street, boasting, "My name is 'Rowser Bill,' and I have come to Oklahoma City to start a graveyard." After several days of this, the men decided to ship "The Shooting Man" to Texas. While waiting for the train, they left him tied to a cottonwood limb. When they returned, they found him hung and claimed the rope about his neck had shrunk in the night's dampness. A speedily impaneled jury agreed. So Bill was buried, the first in Oklahoma City, thus he started a graveyard as he had predicted.

It was a strange way for Paul Curry to put himself through school. He was 18 that day when Henry Starr's gang of outlaws rode into Stroud and pulled off a double bank robbery. As they herded the frightened bankers and clerks ahead of them, the youth told another citizen if he wasn't going to use his gun, he would. Taking the weapon, Curry opened fire on the outlaws. He downed Starr and Lewis Estus, both of whom were captured, and immediately wired Governor Williams, claiming the $1,000 reward. Curry said he would put the money into his education fund.

The Dalton brothers were among the most notorious outlaws in Oklahoma history. From Kingfisher County, they established a reign of terror in Indian Territory during the late 1800s, robbing banks and trains. They met their end at Coffeyville, Kansas, on October 5, 1892, while attempting to hold up two banks at once. During the ensuing fight, four of the bandits and four citizens were killed. Oddly enough, Grat, Bob, and Frank Dalton had been U.S. deputy marshals before they took to the outlaw trail and Emmett Dalton usually tagged along unofficially.

She held a two-fold office in Norman as District Clerk and Deputy U.S. Marshal. In March 1893, when Marshal Grimes telegraphed there were two desperadoes badly wanted in Oklahoma City for perjury, unable to find a male deputy, she put on her bonnet and took the train. She found the two men in a saloon, and unarmed, called them outside and said they were under arrest. Considering it a joke, they allowed her to handcuff them. On March 11, she took them to Guthrie where they were convicted. She was Miss Ada Curnutt, 24, the daughter of a Methodist clergyman.

Nelson Ellsworth (Zip) Wyatt, alias Dick Yeager, rode with the Bill Doolin gang and had a reputation for stealing cattle and robbing banks. In August 1895, a posse found him critically wounded near Marshall. He was taken to Enid where he died on September 6. After his death he was buried in an unmarked grave near the present day Owen K. Garriot and Van Buren roads. Later a housing project was built on the site. A marker at the downtown courthouse square states the outlaw's body is still there.

Frontier justice often took a strange turn. During the hectic days following the settling of Oklahoma City, a tough gambler named George "Satan" Shields, heard that several members of the Wolf gang from Lexington were in town to get a friend of his. Shields purchased a hickory axe handle, then found the gang of killers in the Black and Rogers Saloon and proceeded to mop up on them. When the battle ended, the six men lay unconscious on the floor. They were taken before Police Judge Ben Miller, who fined them $100 each—on a charge of attempting suicide.

"Sandtown" was known as the place where all vices associated with liquor ran rampant. It sprang into being soon after the Run of 1889, on a sandbar in the Canadian River between Lexington and Purcell. The river served as the boundary between wet Oklahoma Territory and the dry Chickasaw Nation. Numerous makeshift saloons operated here. Periodic rises in the river washed the saloons away, but the owners quickly rebuilt. Sandtown existed until March 11, 1897, when outlawed by the fourth Oklahoma Legislature.

Following the Run of 1889, it stood to reason that the saloon closest to the dry side of the boundary line could capture the most liquor trade. With this in mind, Fred Ferry built his saloon on a flatboat anchored in the Canadian River between Lexington and Purcell. Each time the river came up, the saloon washed downriver. The saloon operated from October 1890 to September 1892, when it sailed away again. It lodged in a bend of the river, a couple of miles south of town, where it remained, thus ending the career of the infamous "City of Purcell."

Until that ill-fated day in 1893, things looked promising for this small town. True, a certain lawless element of society was being attracted to the town because o." its proximity to the Kansas border, but the young men didn't bother the townfolks and the money they spent here was welcome. Then on September 23, a covered wagon pulled into town carrying a posse. During the gun battle which erupted, three of the lawmen and two citizens were killed. After that the citizens began to move away. Today, little remains of once booming Ingalls.

Temple Houston was one of the most flamboyant figures in Northwestern Oklahoma. Ladies adored him and men feared him. He was a deadshot with a gun. As an attorney, he was a spellbinder with his silver-tongued oratory. Edna Ferber was so enamored by him that she patterned Yancy Cravat, the hero of her novel, *Cimarron*, after him. The son of General Sam Houston, Temple had moved to Woodward shortly after it was established to develop his own reputation. He was reportedly being groomed as the first governor of Oklahoma when he met an untimely death in 1905.

They knew him as "Red" Kelly. He blew into Oklahoma City toward the end of 1903 after serving 10 years in prison for murder in Creede, Colorado. Picked up once as a "suspicious character," he carried two guns and bragged he was "out gunning for a policeman." On the night of January 13, 1904, he and Policeman Joe Burnett tangled. They fought for 15 minutes in the street with no one, not even another policeman, offering to help Burnett. Finally, Burnett shot and killed Ed Kelly, the man who had murdered Bob Ford, the killer of Jesse James.

It was vigilante work at its worst. The trouble began on December 29, 1898, when two drunken Indians raped and killed a white woman near Maud. A vigilante mob of over 300 men rounded up dozens of young Seminoles and questioned them. On January 8, the unlawful mob burned two of the young Indians alive at the stake. Congress appropriated $20,000 to track down those responsible for this atrocity. Deputy marshals arrested 69 suspects. Later, witnesses proved the vigilantes had killed two innocent men in their eagerness for revenge.

He gained fame as the "Petrified Man," but in the beginning he was a little known Oklahoma outlaw. Reportedly, he was killed in 1911 and no one claimed his body. So an enterprising undertaker embalmed his body and sold it to a carnival owner. For nearly 60 years the mummified man traveled about the country, then someone spotted him in a Long Beach funhouse and determined he was real. After his identity was established, he was brought back to Oklahoma in 1977, and now lies beside his outlaw friend, Bill Doolin, in Guthrie's Summit View Cemetery, Elmer McCurdy.

On August 2, 1917, an army of 400 poor tenant farmers rode toward Saskawa in Ponotoc County, intent on plundering the town for arms, then overthrowing the federal government. Their leader, a member of the Working Class Union, had convinced them all their economic troubles were being caused by the nation's involvement in the world war, so the solution was to get out of the war and to reject the draft. But the rebel farmers were met by 1,000 posse members, and their leader, H. H. "Rube" Munson, was jailed. So it failed, "The Green Corn Rebellion."

It was the worst single incident of racial violence in our nation. It began on May 30, 1921, when a black man was accused of molesting a white girl on a Tulsa elevator. *The*

Tulsa Tribune carried an inflammatory story that afternoon. Shortly, a white lynch crowd of 2,000 gathered at the courthouse. A group of 50 black men arrived to help protect the prisoner. Suddenly, the fight was on. Before it was over 38 lives were lost (some say 300), hundreds were injured, 1,115 residences were burned in the black community, and $1.5 million worth of property was looted.

No one thought it could happen here, yet it did. When 65 state representatives attempted to convene at the state capitol on September 26, 1923, to impeach the governor, they were turned back by armed guards. Machine guns were trained on the grand jury room at the County Courthouse and on City Hall. The governor had placed the entire state under martial law, charging insurrection by the Klu Klux Klan. On October 2, 1923, voters supported the legislators right to assemble, 5-1. Subsequently, John Walton was impeached on 11 charges of abuse of power.

Edwin DeBarr, one of the University of Oklahoma's first professors, was a member of the Klu Klux Klan. He came to OU in 1890 and established the school of pharmacy and school of petroleum engineering. The OU chemistry building was built and dedicated to him in 1917. In 1922, the OU regents censured him for his KKK activities, and dismissed him in 1923. He was a grand dragon of Oklahoma and in 1924 served as national chaplain of the Klan. Intermittent attempts were made to remove his name from the chemistry building but this was not accomplished until 1988.

During the 1920s, the Klu Klux Klan was particularly active in Tulsa. Klan No. 2 claimed a membership of 3,200 in 1921, and the Women of the Klu Klux Klan formed here in June 1923. Tulsa was also one of the few places in the nation where the Junior Klu Klux Klan existed. This order, founded in 1924, was open to white boys from 12 to 18 years of age. The golden era of the Klan ended shortly after when legislators passed a law making it illegal for members of any secret organization to conceal their identity with a mask or hood, on any street, road, or highway.

Bonnie Parker and Clyde Barrow were among the most sought after desperados in Oklahoma during the 1930s. Numerous legends about them existed. One, however, was entirely unfounded: Bonnie Parker was never a cigar smoking moll. A Joplin, Missouri, photographer later confessed he was responsible for the image. Given an undeveloped roll of film that had been found in a room Bonnie and Clyde had occupied, and after making the prints, he penned in a cigar on one. That photograph was much copied until the cigar became as much a part of Bonnie Parker as her gun.

On July 22, 1933, Charles E. Urschel, an Oklahoma City millionaire oil man, and a friend were kidnapped as they sat playing bridge. The friend was soon released but Urschel was blindfolded, driven hundreds of miles away, and kept captive for eight days. On payment of $200,000 in ransom, he was released. Shortly after, he helped locate his kidnapper. He distinctly remembered a plane passed directly over the hideout twice daily at 9 a.m. and 5:45 p.m. With this information, officers pinpointed the spot and arrested "Machine Gun" Kelly.

"Pretty Boy" Floyd was one of the FBI's most wanted men, leaving a trail of destruction during his bank robbing career during the late 1920s and early 1930s. It was said he robbed only from the rich and gave to the poor. Soon he became a folk hero. When he was killed by the FBI in 1934, 20,000 people attended his funeral at Sallisaw, and souvenir hunters chipped away at his headstone. Strangely enough, chased by the law most of his adult life, Floyd was buried at

Akins, surrounded on three sides by the graves of former lawmen, all relatives.

It was an unprecedented action. The whole top floor of the prison dorm was turned into educational space. For the warden believed that the more education the "boys" had the less likely they'd be to get in trouble again when free. The school became accredited and compulsory for all who had not finished the eighth grade. In addition, the warden placed a Bible in every cell, established a prison library, and taught the inmates table manners. Serving from 1927 to 1934 at Granite State Reformatory, she was Oklahoma's only woman warden, Clara Waters.

ESTABLISHING THE BOUNDARIES

Many flags have flown over Oklahoma.

They called the Panhandle "No Man's Land." A governmental orphan, this strip of land, 167 miles long and 34 miles wide, evolved through a number of boundary settlements. Texas claimed the area following its war of independence in 1845 but relinquished it in the Compromise of 1850. For 29 years the land was known as a haven for outlaws. In 1887, law-abiding citizens organized the Cimarron Territory and attempted to govern themselves, but finally, on May 2, 1890, Congress created the Territory of Oklahoma and attached the Panhandle to it.

Greer County once belonged to Texas. For 30 years the Lone Star State operated courts and schools here, collected taxes, and handed out land certificates to Civil War veterans. The original treaty with Spain had established the boundary between Mexico and the United States as the main channel of the Red River. When Texas took over, the state assumed this meant the north fork of the stream. However, in 1896, the U.S. Supreme Court ruled the south fork was the main channel, so Oklahoma owned the area, not Texas, and thousands of settlers lost their land grants.

The I. F. C. Moss family lived in the same house near Hollis for 45 years, yet resided in one territory, two states, and three counties. The confusion began in 1819 when emmissaries treating with Spain for certain parts of today's Oklahoma and Texas, used a map which placed the boundary line 90 miles east of its present location. A survey of 1859 placed the line 4,000 feet too far west. A 1902 survey moved it 3,600 feet east. It wasn't until 1929 that a geodetic surveyor, appointed by the U.S. Supreme Court, finally fixed the proper location of the 100th Meridian.

SETTLING THE TOWNS

The settlers were independent thinkers when it came to naming their towns.

Several stories are told about the origin of the name of the Cherokee capital. The most colorful version states that after the Eastern Cherokees arrived in Indian Territory about 1836, they decided that several of them would meet at a certain time to select a site and a name for the capital of the new government. Heavy rain fell the day before the meeting, and only two Cherokees managed to reach the site. They waited most of the day for the others, finally one said, "Tah-le-ya-quah," meaning two are enough, and so the name was chosen, Tahlequah.

Oddly enough, this town was named for a family of outlaws. During the 1880s, five brothers lived in a dugout in the brush on Wildhorse Creek, near the Chisholm Trail. At night they would raid the herds being driven up from Texas and drive the longhorns into the brush. A few days later they would bring the cattle back, pretending they had found them, and collect a reward. But finally the cattlemen became suspicious, set a trap for them and wiped out the outlaw band. The town which grew up at the site of their dugout adopted their name, the infamous Marlow brothers.

This town in southwestern Oklahoma was said to have been founded during a flood in 1891. Nearby Bitter Creek had roared out of its banks, inundating the surrounding area. The settlers grabbed what possessions they could and rushed up the slope of the hill where the town now stands. Here, out of reach of the high water, they established a camp, living in dugouts until they could haul in sufficient lumber to build homes. Someone suggested a name for the town, stating the word meant "higher ground." So it was accepted: Altus.

Can census figures be trusted? In 1893, the citizens of Moore decided to incorporate as a town. But first they were told they had to conduct a census. The story is related that when the two census workers were about to complete their count, totaling 99 residents, a jackass belonging to grocer Bud Cottrell began braying down the street. "Let's count him in to make it an even 100," proposed William G. Jury, one of the census takers. They did, and Moore's first population figure was officially recorded as 100.

It's an intriguing name for a town. In the beginning this crossroads settlement at the edge of the Panhandle was known as Nye. But the old man who owned the general store there didn't carry much stock and when asked for something often replied, "I'm slap out of that." One day a newcomer offered to buy his store so he could get himself slap out of there. The old man quickly agreed. The new owner erected the biggest sign in town on the front of his store with its new name. Soon Nye lost its identity and the community became known by the store's name: Slapout.

This town has a split personality. Some of its 1,200 residents live in one state and some in another. The town maintains two sets of municipal officials and two school boards. Students attend school in two states. Before the boundary was moved 473 feet south in 1934, it actually went through the train depot. It is possible for some residents to walk in their front door in one state and out their back door into another. Established on March 18, 1902, on the Oklahoma-Texas border in the Panhandle, this town is, what else, Texhoma.

Claremore first gained fame as a spa. In 1903, when oil drillers struck artesian water northeast of town, they left the well uncapped. The water seeped into nearby Dog Creek, and residents claimed the water peeled paint off houses, turned gold black, and smelled bad. It was also said to have cured a dog of the mange, and a woman of stomach problems. Within a year, a railroad conductor built the town's first bathhouse. Five others followed, capitalizing on the "Radium Water." Today, only the Hotel Will Rogers remains, a relic of the old watering hole.

Sulphur began as a spa, too, clustered around a group of sulphur and bromide springs. These waters, exponents claimed, could cure anything from rheumatism to catarrah. Located on the Chickasaw Indian reserve in the Arbuckle Mountains, the town was moved twice after the land became a national reserve. Sick folks still flocked here to stroll from their boarding houses and hotels to sip at the springs. In 1907, the Chamber of Commerce claimed 58,000 visitors. Today, with its mineral wells running low, Sulphur's mineral water industry is no more.

It was the town that refused to die. Successive blows of hard luck would have destroyed one of lesser fortitude. Its buildings burned a half-dozen times in the first half of the 19th century. A gas-stove manufacturing plant, established after WWI, failed, likewise the plow plant which took its place, and then the airplane factory which followed. A hardwood planing mill and packing plant failed too. In 1927, a tornado raked the town, but it still didn't give up. Located on the site of Choteau's old trading post, it chose a new name signifying its spirit: Okay.

If you think daylight savings time is confusing, consider the plight of those in Kenton. It is the only town in Oklahoma not on Central Standard Time. Located in the northwestern corner of the Panhandle, sometime in the late 1920s local businessmen decided to set their clocks to Mountain Standard Time. This has worked out fairly well as most locals shop in New Mexico and obtain their television programs from Colorado, both Rocky Mountain States. But their children go to school in Boise City on Central Time, thus creating confusion for many households.

In 1929, a planned suburban community was built east of Oklahoma City. Its concept combined country living with an opportunity for a second income. Each of the 96 houses had an identical chicken coop in the backyard. The residents could sell eggs and poultry through the community cooperative. At first everything went fine, then one day a chicken wholesaler shipped a diseased flock into the colony. Within a few days, every flock was infected and the chicken empire crumbled. Nothing was left but shattered dreams in Nicoma Park.

Things looked promising for Berwyn. A movie star had bought a 1,200 acre ranch near town. He planned to spend $250,000 on improvements, and the town was to be renamed in his honor. On November 16, 1941, 35,000 visitors poured into the hamlet of 227 persons. The governor spoke on a nationwide radio broadcast, and newsreel cameramen and photographers covered the event. Then three weeks later, the nation plunged into WWII. The movie star entered the service and sold his property, leaving nothing behind but his name, Gene Autry.

OIL BOOM DAYS

Oklahoma became a leader in oil production.

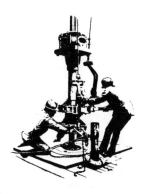

Even before the discovery of the first oil well in Indian Territory in 1859, abundant evidence of petroleum existed in the land. Oil seeps, or oil springs, were often reported by the Five Civilized Tribes. They valued these "medical springs" for their supposed curative powers which were reputed to heal any disease known to man. Some of the Indians bottled the smelly liquid and sold it as an elixir. Others drove a tube or gun barrel into the ground and then ignited the escaping gas, which furnished both heat and light.

As so often happens, the discovery of oil in the state was accidental. In 1859, Lewis Ross, who was a brother to Cherokee Chief John Ross, was engaged in the profession of salt making. One day he sank a deep well near the Grand Saline in what is today Mayes County. It was his hope that he could increase production by opening up a new source of salt water. Instead, he struck oil at about 700 feet. His accidental find opened up the search for oil in Indian Territory, and this eventually led to Oklahoma becoming a leader in oil production.

On April 15, 1897, the Nellie Johnson No. 1 blew in near Bartlesville. Oklahoma's largest oil well to date, it was the state's first practical producer. But the owner, Michael Cudahy, could not market the oil because there were no roads in the area, no pipelines, nor rail facilities. So he sealed the well, hoping time would solve the problem. However, the seal leaked, spilling oil into the Caney River. One cold night, ice skaters built a bonfire near the river to keep warm. The crude oil in the river ignited, and the Nellie Johnson No. 1 went up in flames.

Many of the Indians who most forcefully fought removal and individual allotment were placed on the worst lands in Oklahoma. Among these were the Osages, who somehow, in spite of allotment, had managed to retain all their mineral rights, even though politicians had been aware some oil explorations had been carried out in the Osage country. Ironically, these lands soon proved to contain enormous pools of petroleum. When the oil burst from the ground during the early 1900s, the Osages found themselves among the richest people in the world.

Gib Morgan was a legendary hero of the Oklahoma oil fields during their earliest days. He was said to have an oil rig so tall it had to be hinged to let the sun and stars go by. He could solve any problem with Yankee ingenuity, assisted by Big Toolie, a giant tool dresser, and Strickie, a mile-long boa constrictor that he had encountered while drilling in South America. A champion of the rotary rig crews, this make believe character was the creation of an oil field worker who gave the driller his own name.

The rotary rig drillers in the Oklahoma oil fields also had their legendary hero. He was Paul Bunyan, imported from the Northwoods. A jack-of-all-trades, this monumental giant usually solved his problems with his herculean strength. He boasted he could dig a hole with a stick faster than a crew could with a drilling rig. He was credited with developing many of the tools and practices used in the oil field. He was said to have a rig so big it was hinged in the middle to let the moon go by, and the derrick man only came down twice a month on payday.

All Oklahoma wildcatters had a favorite trick for finding oil. Some placed their faith in the divining rod. Others claimed remarkable success with the "doodlebug." One man relied on a giant X-ray machine which he said could see the oil in the ground. Another man said he could sense oil by the tension in his neck; still another wore a jug of oil around his neck and claimed to receive a jolt of electricity when he passed over oil. But most wildcatters relied upon the theory that "close is best," drilling as close as they could to the last producer.

Wewoka's name became a catch phrase in the late 1890s. During the boomtown days in the Oklahoma oil fields, the town had the only railroad sidetrack between Oklahoma City and Little Rock, Arkansas. Misguided freight often sat there for months before being found. This happened so often the Rock Island railroad automatically stamped all communications concerning lost shipments with the statement: "Search the Wewoka Switch." Before long, anyone having difficulty was said to be "caught in the Wewoka switch."

Harry Sinclair didn't have a bit of business sense, said his neighbors. After losing his father's drug store in Kansas, he drifted to Ochelata. In 1903, he accidentally shot his left foot and part of it was amputated. Then his fortune changed. Investing a $5,000 insurance policy in oil derrick foundations, he reinvested his profits in oil leases. By 1905, he had 1,000 producing wells. Later he headed 62 oil companies, was partner in a Tulsa bank, chairman of a million dollar consolidation, owned a Kentucky Derby winner, and a share in the St. Louis Browns.

Oklahoma's first commuter train was fondly called the "Coal Oil Johnny" by those who rode it. Following the discovery oil at Glenn Pool in 1905, the population of Tulsa grew rapidly as workers poured into the city. To facilitate the transportation of these workers to the outlying oilfields, civic leaders promoted a special train which pulled about 15 coaches. The train left Tulsa each morning, letting the workers off at the various oil fields in the area, and picked them up again in the evening for the return trip to Tulsa.

Ruby Darby's fame preceded that of Sally Rand. "Darb" played the Oklahoma boomtowns during the oil rush days and later the army camps. She was rumored to have "stripped at the drop of a driller's hat," "ridden a hoss completely nekkid one day in the mud-and-oil splashed streets of Kiefer," and "danced bare-skinned on a tool shack roof as men tossed silver dollars at her feet." One of the first and greatest blues singers, her name became synonymous in the fields for something special or great. "That's a real darb," people were apt to say in appreciation.

It was a most curious sight. In 1915, during the Creek County oil boom days, this small village of 35 people exploded into a population of 10,000. Officials imbued the town and all the streets with Irish sounding names. Merchants on the main thoroughfare painted their buildings green. The postmaster tinted the postage stamps green, and the two editors titled their newspapers the *Brogue* and the *Blarney*. An enterprising salesman even peddled a Blarney Stone. But the luck of the Irish failed. The wildcatters moved away and Shamrock fell into ruin.

Clark Gable's father despaired Clark would ever become a he-man. The two hit the Oklahoma oil fields in the mid-1920s, and Clark was unable to handle the heavy work. He went to work in Tulsa as an accountant but couldn't handle the math. He drifted back into the oil fields, where he began to develop an excellent physique. When he told his father he wanted to become an actor, they had a bloody fist fight and didn't speak to each other for years. But Clark went on to Hollywood where he became a star, recreating many of the roles he had performed in Oklahoma.

Following the discovery of the Oklahoma City oil field in 1928, drilling rapidly moved northward. The Oklahoma City Council passed an ordinance limiting the number of oil wells within the city limits. Oilmen complained about these restrictions, then in October 1935, oil was discovered just east of the State Capitol. Ignoring the City Council, Governor E. W. Marland, himself an oilman, called out the state militia and allowed drilling on the State Capitol complex. These oil wells still remain on capitol grounds, the only instance in the nation.

That day in March 1930 began quietly enough. Drillers were just completing a promising addition to the Oklahoma City oil field when suddenly the well blew. For 11 days it ran wild, spraying oil on Oklahoma City, and when the wind changed, as far south as Norman, 11 miles away. Film and radio news crews rushed to the scene. Famed war correspondent Floyd Gibbons flashed bulletins to the world twice a day. Finally workers closed the well in, and it went on to produce 2,000 barrels of oil an hour, the infamous Mary Sudik No. 1.

For years people speculated as to why Phillips Petroleum Company picked the number 66 for its trademark. Truth is, it was due to a coincidence. Time was running out in the name selection process, when one day a company official was riding in a car using the new Phillips gasoline. He commented to the driver, "This car goes like 60 on our new gas." The driver glanced at the speedometer. "Sixty nothing, we're doing 66." And it so happened they were on Highway 66. So, at the next conference the story was told, and the trademark quickly became Phillips 66.

The Oklahoma City oil field proved a puzzle to oil men. They could find no more oil adjacent to the discovery well. In 1930, a young Phillips Petroleum Company geologist set out to unravel the mystery. He found pockets of oil had been uplifted in the past, then worn down by erosion. He suggested Phillips purchase drilling sites farther away. No pool had been developed before, based strictly on geological information, but Phillips took the gamble and gained control over the Wilcox sand production, the richest in the field, thanks to Dean A. McGee.

In 1931, Oklahoma was producing more oil than the nation could consume. Then the East Texas oil field blew in, adding to the problem of overproduction. When oil dropped to 16 cents a barrel, Governor William Murray vowed to save the oil industry. He declared a state of emergency and called out the militia to shut down all production in Oklahoma until the price of oil returned to one dollar a barrel. Texas continued production though, and Murray finally gave in when oil reached 75 cents a barrel.

Tulsa, which was to become known as the Oil Capital of the World, began as a small Creek village in a bend of the Arkansas River. Following the Civil War, the cattle industry dominated the town; but in 1901, when oil was discovered at nearby Red Fork, the site quickly became a focal point for oil and gas exploration. Oddly, while maintaining strict prohibition against drilling within the city limits, Tulsa's only well resulted in 1934 at the International Petroleum Exposition when a crew demonstrating drilling equipment accidentally made a strike.

W. W. Marland became one of the richest oil men in Oklahoma. His second mansion, begun in 1925, cost $5.5 million, had 55 rooms, 12 bathrooms, a ballroom with an $80,000 ceiling of gold, and two chandeliers worth $15,000 each. The mansion was situated on 2,500 acres northeast of Ponca City, and the grounds featured polo stables, playing fields, a game refuge, five lakes, an art gallery, and an olympic size swimming pool. In addition, Marland built a kennel for his hunting dogs and imported foxes so his guests could participate in authentic English fox hunts.

The story is often told that oil baron Frank Phillips had a servant who was himself a millionaire. Of Japanese descent, Dan Matani was Phillips' personal valet at the time Pearl Harbor was bombed. On the East Coast, Phillips had to hide Matani in a hotel room and obtain special permission to fly him back to Bartlesville. It is said Matani made his million listening to stock market tips while in Phillips' employment. After the war, he returned to Japan, but he had gotten used to American life and came back to resume his valet position with Phillips.

BUSINESS AND INDUSTRY

From gold rushes to a variety of inventions, Oklahoma has been progressive.

Gold! The Wichita Mountains rang with the word, and legends abound of lost Spanish mines. The first gold rush here occurred in 1849. In July 1881, a chunk of almost pure silver set off a second stampede. By 1895, hundreds of prospectors were swarming onto the Kiowa-Comanche lands in spite of military protection. Mining camps mushroomed, and smelters rumbled day and night. Millions of dollars were taken from the rocky hillsides during the next 20 years. Today, only decaying ruins and one lone store at Meer give testimony of the great Oklahoma gold rush.

It was a proud day for Oklahomans when the St. Louis Worlds Fair ended in 1893. C. G. "Gristmill" Jones, Oklahoma City businessman who had built the first flour mill in Oklahoma Territory, won the premium for the best patent flour. In addition, the tallest corn at the fair measured seventeen-feet two-inches, and was produced on fertile ground near Norman. In a display of Oklahoma pride, next morning during a special ceremony, ringing the new Liberty Bell, the enterprising Oklahomans flew their flag from the corn stalk.

William Wrigley was the world's largest manufacturer of chewing gum. He left home at the age of 11, and at 13 began making soap and baking powder in Chicago. From there he drifted to Guthrie were he invented his first chewing gum at 113 North Division Street. For several years he made a number of different flavors, then in 1899, he introduced a new flavor, "Spearmint." The gum failed to impress the public until he spent $84,000 on advertising in 1907. Growing rich from his venture, in 1919, he bought Catalina Island, where he died in 1932.

The Miller Brothers famous 101 Ranch boasted the largest wheat field in Oklahoma Territory. Located in Kay County, it covered 5,000 acres. In 1899, it took workers four hours to make the six-mile trip around the field. The 24 binders, pulled by horses, cut a swath 150 feet wide. A team of men followed on foot to shock the wheat while two machinists rode beside the binders, ready to cope with any mechanical difficulty. Employed in shifts, more than 200 men with 300 horses and mules worked around the clock during harvest time.

The Krebs-McAlester coal fields were termed the melting pot of Oklahoma. With the development of the coal mines in 1873, skilled miners were imported to work them. Among these were those of English, Irish, Scotch, and Welsh descent. The first Italians arrived in 1874, the Lithuanians in 1875, and the Slovaks in 1883. A colony of French came in 1889 and later Mexican miners arrived. Each group clung to its own folkways and customs. Mine owners complained about the number of holy days, holidays, fiestas, and other celebrations which the miners took.

In October 1895, gold was discovered eight miles northeast of Norman. Edwin Debarr, chemistry professor at the University of Oklahoma, assayed the rock taken from the claim and stated it was very rich. A stampede headed for the location, and claims were staked over a large area. A few days later news came of still richer finds. A test lot of ore was shipped to Argentine, Kansas, and the following spring, a mining company brought in heavy equipment. Activity flourished for a few months, then the gold disappeared.

George Chase Beidler was 11 years old when he arrived with his family at Oklahoma Station, April 11, 1889. His father, G. A. Beidler, had been appointed first postmaster of Oklahoma City. In the early 1900s, Chase worked as a clerk in an Oklahoma City asbtract office. Growing weary copying documents by hand, he developed a photographic process for quick copying. He called his invention a "Rectigraph." In 1906, he founded the Rectigraph Co. of Oklahoma, which he moved to Rochester, New York, in 1909. Eventually this company became the Xerox corporation.

Charles Page had a heart as big as his millionaire purse strings. When he was ten his father died and he never forgot how hard his mother had to work to support her family of eight. When Charles eventually struck it rich in oil, he determined to do something for the poor. In 1908 he bought 160 acres of land seven miles west of Tulsa. Here he built a home for widows and orphans, and literally constructed a town around it, developing a refinery, glass plant, textile mill, steel plant, and a host of other industries, to support his Sand Springs Home Interests.

Raymond A. Young, a partner in T.G.&Y., had an unusual way of determining if a prospective employee was suitable for the job. He would accompany the man to the restroom and if he used three paper towels to dry his hands, he stood no chance at the job. If he used two towels he got a lecture on economy, and if he used only one towel he had a good chance of being hired. For Young believed a man who was unconcerned about little things would waste pennies, and this could spell the difference between a profitable or unprofitable store.

J. C. Penney, the only non-Oklahoman inducted into the Oklahoma Hall of Fame gallery in 1971, also had an unusual method for testing a prospective employee. He had begun in the drygoods business in 1904. He sold only for cash and at the lowest possible markup. This meant his managers had to know their exact overhead and operational costs. So his standard test was to dine with a prospective employee. If the man salted his food without tasting it first, to Penney that meant he reached conclusions without considering all the evidence and so he wasn't hired.

C. R. Anthony once worked for the Wewoka Trading Company for $1 a month. Eventually he managed a store for J. C. Penney. There he learned the wisdom of selling goods at a minimum markup, and of obtaining profits through volume sales. Until then the whole attitude of selling had been to see how much one could get for an item. He opened his first store in Cushing on September 1, 1922. This grew into a chain of more than 300. Each store was noted for its quality merchandise, and courtesy and service of the salespeople, reflecting the owner's personality.

T.G.&Y. was destined to become one of the nation's best known chain stores. Its roots developed in 1935 when three Oklahoma variety store owners formed a wholesale company called Central Merchandising. A year later, they opened their first joint retail store in Norman under the new name of T.G.& Y. The famous trademark was derived from their initials, chosen in order of their ages. The founders of this famous variety store were Rawdon E. Tomlinson of Frederick, E. L. "Les" Goslin of Cordell, and Raymond Young of Kingfisher.

The nation's first parking meter was invented in Oklahoma City in 1935 by a former newspaperman. A member of the Oklahoma City Chamber of Commerce traffic committee, Carl Magee was given the job of trying to solve the downtown parking problem. He came up with an ingenious method of regulating the parking time with a metering device. The first parking meter was installed at Park Avenue and Robinson Street on July 16, 1935. It remained in service for one year, then it was donated to the Oklahoma Historical Society.

Little did Sylvan N. Goldman dream he was about to change the shopping habits of Americans, that day in 1955. He stood in his Humpty Dumpty store in Ardmore observing how women had to shop with their groceries in one arm and a child in the other. Wouldn't it be wonderful, he thought, if they had a cart in which to place their groceries? At first he couldn't get women to use the carts so he hired others to push them about until they got the idea. Today, a bronze statue in the Oklahoma City Kirkpatrick Center commemorates the inventor of the shopping cart.

It was to be Oklahoma's great experiment in providing homes and jobs for the needy. During the early 1970s, the Office of Economic Opportunity purchased land near Caney, and planted hybrid grape cuttings. Then it moved in mobile homes and offered free twenty-acre homesteads to low income families. This utopian project was beset by troubles from the beginning and quietly died a couple of years later. However, the grapevines lived on and began to produce. Eventually, the site became Oklahoma's only full-scale commercial vineyard and winery, Cimarron Cellars.

Pearl farming is one of Oklahoma's little known industries. In the 13th century, men learned to grow cultured pearls by introducing a foreign object into a mollusk. The industry depends upon a continual source of fresh water mussel shells. Lake Fort Gibson supplies just that, though not on as large a scale as a few years ago before the lake was poisoned. Each year divers harvest tons of mussels for Japanese pearl farmers who cut and tumble the shells to bead size, then insert them in pampered oysters, which develop cultured pearls in about seven years.

The peanut is Oklahoma's third largest cash crop, and almost half of the state's production is grown in Caddo County. The lentil was discovered by the Spanish in South America, made its way to Africa in trade, and was brought to this country by African slaves who called it goober peas. George Washington Carver developed more than 300 uses for the product, and today our nation consumes more than 1 billion pounds of peanuts a year. But strangely enough, European countries have never acquired a taste for the peanut.

The Woodward Iodine Plant produces 25 percent of the nation's iodine supply. Drillers were looking for oil in 1975 when they discovered a formation deep in the earth that contained highly concentrated iodine solutions. Their company built a refinery eight miles north of Woodward, and drilled 14 wells into the formation, some 7,000 feet below. Here in the Morrow layer, they pumped the rich iodine brine to the surface at the rate of two million gallons a day, and extracted the iodine from the brine for medical purposes.

TRANSPORTATION AND COMMUNICATION

Oklahoma served as the crossroads of the nation.

The Santa Fe Trail is the oldest highway in Oklahoma. No signposts pointed the way for travelers, yet thousands found their way along it. Leaving Independence, Missouri, the trail crossed the rolling prairies of Kansas and entered what is now Cimarron County, 12 miles north of present Keyes, and cut diagonally southwest into New Mexico. From 1820 to about 1880, it was the main thoroughfare to the West. Countless wagons and pack animals left their mark on the trail, which is still visible today, and dozens of passersby scratched their name on Autograph Rock.

The Texas Road was one of the earliest roads in eastern Oklahoma. They all traveled over it, the fur traders, trappers, emigrants, and pioneer settlers. From the Kansas line to Three Forks the road followed the Osage trace. With the coming of trading posts, missions, and Fort Gibson along its length, the road pushed rapidly on toward Texas. The heavy traffic left ruts that still scar the land today. During a six-week count, beginning in March 1845, 1,000 wagons traveled down the Texas Road to cross the Red River.

The *Lucy Walker* was the finest boat on the Arkansas River. She was owned by Joseph Vann, a wealthy half-blood Cherokee from Webbers Falls. In the spring of 1844, Vann was steaming down the Mississippi when he challenged another boat to a race. He ordered his deckhand to stoke the furnace with part of the boat's cargo. Soon black smoke rolled from the twin smokestacks of the paddlewheeler. Suddenly, the boiler exploded, killing all aboard except the deckhand, who leaped overboard, and the boat sank, done in by a barrel of fatty salt pork.

Indian Territory's first commercial telephone line linked Tahlequah, Fort Gibson, and Muskogee in September 1886. Because the line passed over tribal land, the Cherokee council had to grant permission. The council stipulated the line must be built over land too rough for a parallel road, hoping to keep out white settlers. Also, the telephone had to demonstrate it could speak Cherokee as well as English. The first message was relayed to J. S. Stapler's store in Tahlequah. The immortal words? "Hello, who is this?" "This is the devil, I'm coming to get you!"

They called it a "railroad war." The trouble began in 1894 when the Rock Island Railroad decided its passenger train would no longer stop at the south station in Enid, but at the north station. Irate citizens at the south end of town tried several things to stop the train, including shooting at it. On July 13, they resorted to sawing the timber of a railroad trestle in two and wrecked the train. Finally, Congress passed a special law stating that trains must stop where the citizens wanted them to, thus ending the railroad war.

They called him "Flying Machine," for G. W. Thompson of Kingston claimed to have invented a machine which could fly. An expert machinist, he had made some ingenious improvements in cotton gin machinery, but at first no one believed him when he said he had built a machine with wings like an eagle that could actually soar. So on June 6, 1902, he invited 11 prominent Kingston citizens to witness a trial run. Later, all signed an affidavit affirming that the "flying eagle indeed had flown," 18 months before the Wright brothers historic flight at Kitty Hawk.

In 1904, all Oklahoma and Kansas newspapers published only six days a week. Russia and Japan were on the verge of war, and one Oklahoma editor feared it might occur on the weekend and his readers would not receive the news that day. Thus he ordered his staff to work on Sunday. As predicted, war was declared that day. The alert editor quickly published an extra edition which he dispensed in Guthrie and Wichita. Subscriptions poured in, and his paper soon outdistanced all rivals. Today, that paper is still a leader, E. K. Gaylord's *Daily Oklahoman.*

The Rock Island passenger train had been running three hours late when it approached the Cimarron River near Kingfisher, that day in September 1909. Ordinarily dry, this fateful Tuesday the river was at flood stage. But a freight train had just crossed the railroad bridge, so the engineer, Claude "Red" Reeves, saw no reason for concern. Seconds later, with a shrill whistle, the engine and four cars plunged into the river. Four people died in the accident and scores were injured. Today, engine No. 614 still rests in the quicksands of the Cimarron River.

In 1910, the Wichita Falls & Northwestern Railroad built within six miles of Beaver and platted the town of Forgan. This meant certain death to Beaver. The citizens determined to build a connecting line. Almost everyone in town donated labor and money. Several times they offered to give the railroad to the Katy, which now owned the line, but were refused. Then came WWI, the price of wheat soared, and Beaver became an important shipping point. The Katy decided to accept the Beaver railroad, but what was once offered as a gift now cost more than $2 million.

People couldn't believe what they were seeing. Two boys, ages six and ten, making a cross-country trip on horseback from Cross Roads, Oklahoma, to New York? Yet it was true. The two-month adventure occurred in 1910, and they were the sons of a U.S. deputy marshal. Hundreds of people greeted them along the way, and they met Wilbur Wright at Dayton, Ohio, President Taft at the White House, and Teddy Roosevelt at New York. On their return trip, the two boys drove their own Brush runabout. They were the Abernathy kids, Bud and Temple.

It was the first commercial broadcasting station west of the Mississippi and only the third such in the nation. It went on the air early in 1920 with the call letters 5XT, transmitting from the cluttered garage of engineer Earl C. Hull in Oklahoma City. In the beginning, he erratically aired orations, played operatic arias on a windup gramaphone, and read the news and stock market reports from the newspapers. In 1922, the station received a new set of call letters and went on to become a leader in its field, pioneering many firsts, WKY.

Established in 1928, U. S. Route 66 became known as the "Main Street of America." The busy highway began in Chicago and stretched 2,200 miles to end at the Pacific Ocean in Los Angeles. The highway entered Oklahoma's northeast corner, passed its two largest towns, and exited at the Texas border. Thus Oklahoma quickly became the crossroads of America. In the 1930s, the highway became the road of desperation described in John Steinbeck's *The Grapes of Wrath*. Today, it has been surpassed by super highways and was officially abandoned on June 25, 1985.

For a brief time, Waynoka held an important role in cross-country travel. It was a stopping point for Transcontinental Air Transport (TAT) which could move passengers from New York to Los Angeles in a combination rail-air trip of 48 hours. Inaugurated August 7, 1929, TAT brought passengers by air to Waynoka where they caught the train next morning. TAT expanded rapidly, then suddenly it was over. On October 10, 1930, the company merged with Western Air Express to become Trans World Airlines. Seven days later, the Waynoka route was suspended and the town's glory faded.

Wiley Post was a one-eyed aviator from Maysville who began his career in 1921 as a barnstormer. He gained fame in 1931 with his around the world flight in the *Winnie May*. For some time he had planned another record flight, this one of height instead of speed or distance. His plan was to fly into the stratosphere, the near border of space. He climbed to a record height of 55,000 in a single engine Lockheed Vega. For the flight he had designed a "space suit," which became the prototype for the pressurized suits used by today's pilots and astronauts.

Thomas P. Stafford, from Weatherford, is the space program's most experienced astronaut. He has logged over 507 hours in space flight, including pilot of Gemini VI, in December 1965; commander of Gemini IX, June 1966; and commander of Apollo 10, May 1969, during the first flight of the lunar module to the moon. In 1975, he was part of the three-man crew that linked up with the Soviets in space for two days during the Apollo-Soyuz flight. A retired Air Force Lieutenant General, he is the highest-ranking military man to have served as an astronaut.

DUSTBOWL FACTS

*The 1930s proved trying
times for Oklahomans.*

The dust storms of the "Dirty Thirties," were a terrifying sight to the farmers of the Great Plains. They could do nothing but watch their land blow away. Anger overcame them because of the futility of it all. The sunsets were perversely beautiful, filtered through the dust laden sky. For seven years, drought cursed the land and the dust storms raged. Millions of acres lost their topsoil, and thousands of weary farmers moved away. Stricken towns became a familiar sight in Western Oklahoma. But out of this ordeal was born the Soil Conservation program.

On April 29, 1933, a dust storm of unprecedented intensity swept over Western Oklahoma. For two years the storms had ravaged the area, transforming once fertile wheatlands of a region as large as New England into a desert. In February, the savagery of the storms had increased, and on this day the worst storm of all struck. The wall of dust rose 10,000 feet high, and boiled over the horizon on the wings of a gale, engulfing everything. Visibility dropped to zero, traffic halted, breathing became difficult, and chickens went to roost at midday.

The spirit of the Civilian Conservation Corps still lives in many Oklahoma state parks. Organized by the federal government during the Great Depression, the CCC provided useful employment for 3 million young men and helped save the nation's natural resources. Under army supervision, these youths built roads and nurseries, landscaped parks, planted trees, and conserved the countryside. In addition to their room, board, medical care, and educational benefits, the CCC volunteers received $30 a month, of which $25 was sent home to help their families.

On March 18, 1935, the Prairie States Forestry Project planted the first tree in the first shelterbelt in the United States. This occurred on the Horace Curtis farm north of Mangum in Greer County. During the early 1930s, dust storms had attacked the mid-section of the nation in unprecedented fury. When he became president, Franklin D. Roosevelt instituted a number of programs to help control soil erosion. During its eight year history, the forestry project planted in Oklahoma 20 million trees in 2,679 miles of shelterbelts on 5,000 farms.

Not only did Oklahoma citizens have to contend with dust storms and the Depression in 1936, but it was also the hottest year on record. The mercury hit 120 degrees at Alva on July 18. The next day, it reached 120 at Altus. On August 10, Poteau sweltered in a 120 degree temperature, and tied the record again on August 12. Thirty-three people had already died that summer because of the heat, and the crops were burning up, even the cotton, which was a hot weather crop. In those days before air conditioning, many people were forced to sleep outdoors.

BLACKS IN OKLAHOMA

Many black slaves came to Indian Territory with the Five Civilized Tribes and became a part of our heritage.

Some called them "Yellow Legs," others called them the "Buffalo Soldiers" because of their short, wooly hair. All agreed they were hard fighting and disciplined. They were the black soldiers of the army's Ninth and Tenth Cavalry regiments. Organized soon after the Civil War with white officers, they were hardened in the Indian wars then spent four years in Indian Territory trying to keep David L. Payne's ragtag army of Boomers out of the "Promised Land." Ironically, the publicity generated from these conflicts eventually led to the opening of the land.

It is the forgotten holiday, yet in Indian Territory from 1870 to the early 1900s, it was an annual celebration. In Wetumka and Wewoka, freedmen celebrated Emancipation Day on August 4. Indians and white people joined with the blacks in the festivities. On that morning, everybody dressed in their finest clothing and went to town. Here they raised the American flag, fired off a cannon, and crowned the queen of the day, who got to ride the best horse. The last known Emancipation Day celebration was observed in Tuskeegee in 1902.

Bill Pickett, the black cowboy, is credited with inventing bulldogging. He had a strange technique. Piling out of his saddle onto the head of a running steer, he'd grab a horn in each hand and twist until the steer's nose came up. Then he'd grab the steer's upper lip with his teeth, throw up his hands to show he wasn't holding on, and drag beside the steer until the animal went down. Zack Miller, of the 101 Ranch near Ponca City, hired Pickett to work on his road show, where he remained for 30 years. However, the Humane Society made him tone down his act.

E. P. McCabe, the former black state auditor of Kansas, was the founder of Langston, which was heralded as "The Only Distinctively Negro City In America." He planned for the town to become another "Eldorado," a place where the black man could prosper and rule supreme in his own community. He laid out the town on a tract of borrowed land 12 miles northeast of

Guthrie. Agents for the town company sold lots all over the South with the purchase price including a railroad ticket to Guthrie. The deed stipulated title to these lots could never pass to a white man.

On January 14, 1946, Ada Lois Sipuel applied for admission to the School of Law at the University of Oklahoma. The daughter of a Chickasha Methodist minister, her grades were excellent. However, she was denied admission solely because of her race. Her case was taken to the United States Supreme Court. There it was ruled Oklahoma's segregation laws, in regard to higher education, were unconstitutional. This decision affected the pattern of Negro higher education throughout the South, and on June 18, 1949, Ada, now Mrs. Fisher, was finally admitted to OU.

TIMES OF WAR

All wars touched Oklahoma and its people.

The Battle of Honey Creek was the most important battle fought in Indian Territory during the Civil War. The fighting lasted all day. For two years the area had been gripped in a reign of terror. Armed soldiers of the Union and Confederate armies marched back and forth, pillaging, burning, and killing. On this day, July 17, 1863, 3,500 Union soldiers engaged 6,000 Confederate troops on the banks of Elk Creek, 12 miles southeast of Muskogee. The Union lost only 17 men, but the Confederates lost 200 and were forced to retreat.

Brigadier General Stand Watie was the last Confederate officer to surrender following the Civil War. He had signed the

Cherokee treaty for removal from Georgia and Tennessee in 1838, and was marked for death along with three other signers by those who regarded them as traitors, but he escaped. He became a bitter opponent of Chief John Ross, whom he accused of the killings. Committing himself to the Confederate cause, Watie enlisted a regiment of Cherokees. He surrendered at Fort Towson on June 23, 1865, 2½ months after General Lee surrendered at Appomatox.

Roy V. Cashion was the first American soldier to be killed in combat on foreign soil, during the Spanish-American War. He was only 17 when he rode to Guthrie to sign up with the 1st U.S. Volunteer Cavalry in May 1898. Two months later, while storming up San Juan Hill in Cuba with Teddy Roosevelt's Rough Riders, a fatal bullet found Roy. His body was brought home several years later and buried at Hennessey. The state legislature appropriated $1,200 to help provide a monument, and Cashion, in Kingfisher County, was named for him.

When the United States entered World War I, the civil liberties of Oklahoma's German residents were sharply curtailed. Church services, phone and public conversations in German were forbidden. German newspapers were attacked. No German alien could live near a transportation system or military facility. Mob violence intimidated individuals with German names, and burned German businesses. The Oklahoma City Board of Education even banned the word "kindergarten," and legislation prohibited all foreign languages in the classroom from 1919 until 1949.

During World War I, patriotism was the keynote at Norman. Citizens organized a company of home guards, erected a savings bond bank on Main Street, and closed meat markets one day a week to enforce meatless days. In addition, the school board abolished German at Norman High School as a course of study, and the high school was one of the few schools in the state which adopted military drill as part of its curriculum. One hundred and thirty-five students drilled daily under the superintendent of schools, N. H. Edwards.

The nation's only Spanish-American War Veterans' Colony was established in 1936, eight miles south of Wilburton. It was intended as a retirement colony for veterans of that war to help them survive on meager pensions. Later, the bylaws were revised to include all honorably discharged veterans. The non-profit organization purchased 760 acres of land for $1 an acre, and the veterans each paid $10 to join the organization. In 1977, the colony sheltered 60 permanent families and welcomed another 75 on weekends.

In 1942, the nation geared up for war, and a chance encounter by a University of Oklahoma staff member resulted in far reaching benefits for Oklahoma. Savoie Lottinville, OU Press, was on his way to New York to discuss a publishing project with editors, when he met a navy captain on the train. Lottinville mentioned OU's new airfield, and the captain inquired whether OU might be willing to lease it to the navy for the duration of the war. With permission, Lottinville went to Washington, D.C., to discuss the matter. Shortly after, two navy bases were built in Norman.

He called it the Indian Signal Corps. Following the attack on Pearl Harbor, William Karty got the idea of forming the young men at the Fort Cobb CCC camp, where he was director, into an all Indian communication group. He thought the Army might find it useful to communicate in the rare Comanche language. The army agreed and drafted 17 of the youths into a special unit. The young men served in some of the biggest battles in Europe, including the Battle of the Bulge, and some came home with Purple Hearts. They were the "Comanche Code Talkers."

The Great Salt Plains Reservoir Dam stands as a monument to the nation's war hysteria. In 1942, Congress ordered hundreds of Japanese-Americans and a few of German descent shipped inland to internment camps. The prisoners at the camp near Jet, Oklahoma, were forced to build a large dam on the Great Salt Plains, which took three years to complete. The rock face was all hand-laid by the prisoners, and many of them lost their minds because of the inhumanity of their internment. Today, the labor camps are gone, but the scars they left still remain.

Oklahoma's 45th Infantry is probably best known for its fighting in World War II. From out of that same division came two of the best known symbols of that war, Willie and Joe, two average G.I. Joes who were created by cartoonist Bill Mauldin. Mauldin's cartoons first appeared in the pages of the 45th Division's newspaper. As his fame grew, he was promoted to cartoonist for the Army's *Stars and Stripes*. Today, 60 of Mauldin's original cartoons are preserved in the 45th Infantry Division Museum in Oklahoma City.

One of Hitler's most valued possessions was his personal copy of *Mein Kampf*, published in 1935. At the height of World War II, the 45th Infantry Division under General Patton were the first American soldiers to enter Munich. A detachment quickly searched Hitler's apartment in Berichtisgartens, and took possession of some of his personal belongings, including his treasured book and an engraved box containing a half-dozen other copies in various foreign languages. Today, all of these books are in the 45th Infantry Division Museum in Oklahoma City.

Boise City had the distinction of being the only town in the U.S. that was bombed during World War II. The lights were still on in the town square, but most citizens were asleep that July 5, 1944, at 1 a.m., when an airplane droned overhead.

Suddenly, the bombs began to fall. There were six of them, breaking windows and blasting craters. The town square lights went out, and the bomber pilot flew back to Dalhart Flying Field in Texas. Forty miles off course, he had mistaken the town square for the bombing range at Conley, Texas, and dropped his practice bombs.

Following World War II, the University of Oklahoma was inundated by veterans returning to school. The housing situation in Norman became critical, and OU President Dr. George Cross purchased 500 prefabricated houses from a Dallas firm for $1,250,000. These were erected on the OU campus south of Lindsey Street to provide homes for 500 veterans and their families. Some considered the tiny, box-like structures little better than foxholes, and ice froze on the inside walls. A community within a community, it was called "Sooner City."

PART 4. SOCIAL LIFE

ARTS AND ENTERTAINMENT

***Many talented people
have lived in Oklahoma.***

Many blacks came to Oklahoma during territorial days as Indian slaves. From the deep South, they had their own music traditions, and their interest in religion led to the development of Negro spirituals. After emancipation two of these slaves, Uncle Wallis Willis and Aunt Minerva, worked at a Choctaw boarding school near the Red River. A minister liked their songs and sent two of them to the Jubilee Singers at Fisk University in Nashville, who added both songs to their repertoire and made them famous: "Swing Low, Sweet Chariot," and "Steal Away Jesus."

Dr. Brewester Highley was a 43-year-old physician living in a log cabin in Kansas in 1872 when he wrote a new song. The words were printed in a local newspaper in 1873 though the music was not published until 1910. First titled "My Western Home," the song soon became a favorite of cowboys on the cattle trails in Indian Territory, calming the herds on stormy nights. The author moved to Shawnee in 1886, where he died in 1911. He never saw a copy of his song nor received a cent in royalties. He was the author of the classic frontier ballad, "Home On the Range."

Will Rogers was Oklahoma's greatest ambassador. Born near Claremore in 1879, he traveled around the world extolling the virtues of the state in his homespun humor. He made 48 silent films and 20 talkies, and wrote over 2 million words, including a regular newspaper column. A friend of the famous as well as the poor, he never forgot his roots. He was also one of the biggest boosters of air travel though he himself never learned to fly. On August 15, 1935, ironically, he was killed in a plane crash along with Wiley Post at Point Barrow, Alaska.

America's first singing cowboy was a real cowboy. Born on the Ponca reservation in 1890, he was playing southwestern music for large audiences long before commercial recordings and motion pictures became popular. In an attempt to preserve the music of the Old West, he began performing western standards live on radio station KFRU in Bristow in 1924. In keeping with the band's image, all of the band members were real cowboys recruited from different Oklahoma ranches. Travelling widely, they were a hit until they disbanded in 1936, Otto Gray and his Oklahoma Cowboys.

This young woman came to Oklahoma City with her father, who had arrived on the first train when the territory was settled and stayed to build the Skirvin Hotel. At her father's hotel, the young woman learned the art of entertaining. Later she married a wealthy Italian who died after eight years and left her his fortune. Moving to Washington, D.C., she soon gained fame for her lavish parties. The friend of movie stars and presidents, the subject of a Broadway play, "Call Me Madam," she was the "Hostess With the Mostest," Perle Mesta.

Tom Mix might have easily stepped out of a dime store novel, for he was young, slender, dashing, and wore rodeo regalia. An army deserter, he appeared suddenly in Guthrie in 1902. He soon established himself as an expert marksman and pugilist. In 1903, Governor Ferguson stunned everyone by appointing "that fancy-Dan" to lead the Oklahoma Territorial Cavalry Band. Mix starred in the 101 Ranch Wild West Show and served as marshal of Dewey at the height of the oil boom. In 1913, he went to Hollywood where he starred in nearly 400 movies, billed as King of the Cowboys.

Oklahoma's first movie was produced by a Frederick cowboy and starred an unusual cast. The cowboy had won Theodore Roosevelt's admiration during his 1905 trip to the "Big Pasture," for his live wolf-catching abilities. But nobody believed the tale back east, so the cowboy formed a movie company to record his feat. The film starred U.S. deputy marshals Heck Thomas, Bill Tilghman, Chris Madsen, outlaw Al Jennings, and Comanche chief Quannah Parker. After a special showing in the White House, Roosevelt appointed the film's producer to a marshalship: John A. Abernathy.

Belle Isle Park was the brainchild of The Oklahoma Railway Co., owners of the Oklahoma City streetcar lines. The officials felt people would ride their cars if they had someplace worth traveling to. They had built a lake for a generating plant near a spring five miles north of the town near present Classen Circle. In 1910, they added an amusement park which reached the height of its glory in the mid-1920s. As Belle Park's popularity waned, the rides and concessions disappeared, leaving only the lake. This soon silted in and faded away too.

The first notated blues song was not born in New Orleans but in Oklahoma City. Herbert Wand lived in Oklahoma City and played with various jazz musicians at Hallie Richardson's Shoe Shine Parlor on East Second Street. One day in his father's store, Wand was composing a new song when a helper sweeping the floor paused and said, "That song gives me the Dallas blues." Wand liked the title, and he published his song in March 1912, several months before W. C. Handy's "Memphis Blues." Within a matter of weeks, "Dallas Blues" was being played up and down the Mississippi.

Chester Gould made his debut on the bulletin board at Oklahoma A&M College in 1919. Though still in Pawnee High School, he became a regular contributor to the college yearbook. After college graduation, he moved to Chicago where he worked as a reporter. One day in the police station, he watched as a hard-jawed officer hauled a crook to jail and an idea clicked in his mind. He went on to become one of the nation's best known comic strip creators. Often drawing his ideas and characters from the real underworld, he was the creator of "Dick Tracy."

Bob Wills had one of the worst bands imaginable when he first arrived in Oklahoma. It was said none of the musicians could play and all were horribly out of tune. The musicians' local would not allow the band to join the union because none of the members could read music. Nevertheless, Bob Wills and his Texas Playboys began broadcasting over Tulsa radio station KVOO on February 6, 1934. They went on to become one of the best known bands in the nation, developing a new style of music called western swing that is still popular today,

Clarence Nash was one of the world's most famous movie actors, yet few recognized him in person. He was born in Watonga in 1904 and at the age of 13 he began imitating animal sounds for his friends. Eventually, he made his way to Hollywood where he became a spokesman on radio for a local milk company. One night, while he was reciting "Mary Had A Little Lamb" in "duck talk," Walt Disney tuned in and promptly hired him. The young actor debuted in 1934 in Disney's cartoon, "Wise Little Hen." He played the same major role for 50 years as the voice of Donald Duck.

Early acoustic guitars were not loud enough for solo work, nor would they sustain a note. During World War I, Americans had gone wild over Hawaiian music. The Hawaiian's had obtained the guitar from the Portuguese and played it flat on their laps with a slide to fret the instrument. Rural musicians in the United States later adopted this method. But one day in January 1935, Bob Dunn, a Beggs musician, had an idea. He took a standard guitar, built up the bridge, and magnetized the strings. Thus, he invented the first electric guitar.

The Oklahoma City "Blue Devils" were among the best in jazz bands. During the 1920s, they frequented Hallie Richardson's Shoe Shine Parlor on East Second Street. One day in Tulsa, a member of the band heard a piano player on the sidewalk doing a come-on for a show. He liked what he heard and invited the piano player to try out for the "Blue Devils," who hired him. In 1935, when the "Blue Devils" folded, the piano player took the nucleus of the band and formed his own band, which began a revolution in American music. He was Bill Basie with his Count Basie Orchestra.

One summer night in 1927, a young telegraph operator at the Chelsea railroad station was strumming his guitar and singing when Will Rogers strolled in to send a wire. Rogers listened to the young man's song and liked it. He suggested the singer go to New York and try to get on the radio. The telegrapher took his advice only to be told to go back to Oklahoma and gain experience. He made his debut on Tulsa's KVOO in 1928 as "Oklahoma's Yodeling Cowboy," and went on to become the most famous of all the singing cowboys, Gene Autry.

Oklahoma had no greater publicist during the Great Depression than Woody Guthrie, an Okemah-born songwriter and singer. A musical genius, he set his lyrics to other people's tunes. He wrote of the Depression and championed the cause of the migrant people in California. Hailed in New York during the 1940s as one of America's greatest folk singers, he was without honor in his hometown because some people said he was a communist. Ironically, he created some of our best loved songs about our country, "This Land Is Our Land," and "Oklahoma Hills."

Oklahoma produced five of the world's greatest dancers. Reigning during the 1940s and 1950s, they were Marjorie and Maria Tallchief, Marsella Hightower, Yvonne Choteau, and Moscelyne Larkin. Marjorie and Maria were sisters, and all were part Indian. No other area in the world has contributed so many great ballerinas to the stage. To what did they owe their success? Many believed it was the young women's Indian heritage, for the Indians were genetically athletic people and they regarded dancing as a sacred matter.

The musical, *Away We Go*, opened all wrong in New Haven. It had no bawdy jokes, no strip-tease girls. It was based on a play titled *Green Grow the Lilacs*, written by Lynn Riggs, which was termed one of the ten best plays on Broadway during the 1930-31 season. Then after 12 years the folk comedy was revived as a musical and proved an instant flop. But by the time it reached Broadway again, on March 31, 1943, it had a new name, among other revisions. It ran for 2,212 performances, and for 15 years held the record as the longest running musical on Broadway, *Oklahoma!*

Mae Boren Axton became known as "The Queen Mother of Country Music," but in the beginning she was a high school English teacher at Duncan. Then one day in 1956, she met a young, unknown performer to whom she took a liking. When he asked if she would write a song for him, she said yes. So, sitting at her kitchen table with her son Hoyt nearby eating peanut butter sandwiches, Mae penned a song which was to prove a turning point in the evolution of rock and roll. It was "Heartbreak Hotel," which was recorded by Elvis Presley.

Carson & Barnes Circus is the largest tent show in America and the most popular. Spawned in 1960 from the merger of five other shows, all nearly sank at sea when the owner bought a boat, loaded his animals on it, and set sail for Canada, only to have the boat catch fire off Nova Scotia.

Luckily, nothing was lost but one zebra. Today, the circus, last of the big tops, plays a different town every day during its performance season and has its winter quarters at Hugo. Oddly enough, its name stems from no special persons, the owner just happened to like it.

Charles Banks Wilson, a Miami artist, is sometimes better known for his watercolors, book illustrations, and portraits than his paintings. Yet some of his finest work is on display every day in the rotunda of the State Capitol where 300,000 visitors a year view them. His four murals depict 400 years of Oklahoma history. Titled "Discovery and Exploration," "Indian Migration," "Frontier Trade," and "Settlement," they took two years to research and plan, and another two years to paint. Wilson completed them in 1976.

Louis L'Amour was the first novelist to receive the Congressional Gold Medal. Such was usually reserved for the likes of Charles Lindbergh, Thomas Edison, and Jonas Salk. L'Amour grew up at Choctaw and began writing while still living in Oklahoma. The author of 101 books, which sold nearly 200 million copies, he became the champion of the common man on the frontier, and his books were known for their historical accuracy. It was in recognition of this fact that President Reagan presented L'Amour with the Congressional Gold Medal on September 24, 1983.

SPORTS

Sports have always been an important part of Oklahoma.

The first organized baseball game in Indian Territory was played at Krebs with Savannah on July 4, 1882. The game had been invented 30 years earlier by Union army hero Major

General Abner Doubleday and gained popularity during the Civil War. It is supposed soldiers at the early military posts in Indian Territory played the sport, but this was the first recorded game. A crowd of 300 spectators watched that day as "Iron Man" Joe McGinnity led the Krebs team to victory over Savannah, 35-3.

Shortly after giving birth to twins in Pottawatomie County, on May 28, 1887, an Indian mother saw a pathway shimmering in the sun. Considering this an omen, she named one of the boys "Bright Path," and predicted great things for him. The boy led an uneventful life until he was 20, then one day he stopped by his school's athletic field to watch the high jump practice. He astounded the coach when he broke the school's record, and he went on to become the world's greatest athlete, capturing both the pentathlon and decathlon championships at the World Olympics in 1912: Jim Thorpe.

One of the strangest touchdowns in football history occurred during the first game between OU and Oklahoma A&M College, played at Island Park in South Guthrie on November 5, 1904. Cottonwood Creek practically surrounded the playing field, and in those days a loose ball belonged to the team which could recover it, no matter how far out of bounds. During this game, the ball fell into the flooding creek and was swept downstream. Five players leaped into the water after the ball. An OU player managed to capture it and made the touchdown. OU went on to win 75-0.

He was called the "great white hope," who finally took the heavyweight title from Jack Johnson. A giant of a man, Jess Willard stood six-foot-seven inches tall and weighed 240 pounds. He began his boxing career in Oklahoma City while working at the Turf Exchange Saloon at 113 Broadway. He put on boxing gloves for the first time in 1911 at the age of 26 at the newly incorporated Athletic Club. He turned pro two years later. His record stood at 23 wins, 20 by KO; 6 losses, 2 by KO; 1 draw; 5 no-decisions. He lost his title to Jack Dempsey on July 4, 1919, and retired.

Governor Lee Cruce loved a good horse race but he hated racetrack gambling. On April 11, 1914, when Tulsa State Fair promoters defied his orders against open gambling, he called out the National Guard to stop the races. But the manager gave the order for the first race, and the horses surged forward with the militiamen firing over their heads. Both horses and men were ordered shot if a second race was attempted. Later, promoters sued the governor, but the jury said he had a right to call out the militia, the first time martial law was declared in Oklahoma.

The mascot for Oklahoma State University, "Pistol Pete," was modeled after a real person. In the beginning, Oklahoma A&M (now OSU) copied the orange and black colors and the tiger emblem from Princeton University. In 1923, some of the Aggie students said the tiger did not truly represent Oklahoma. One day they saw a 90-year-old veteran of the Old West from Perkins leading a parade, and decided that he was their model. They approached the grizzled cowboy about using his name and likeness for their college emblem. He agreed: Frank "Pistol Pete" Eaton.

They called him the "Indian horse." He was a leggy, black, three-year-old when he broke into the big-time. His owner, a full-blood Indian, had long dreamed of breeding and training a top racing horse. Then the owner became critically ill. But before his death he had a vision that the colt, as yet unborn, would win the Kentucky Derby, and named him. Eventually, when the colt was nominated to run in the Kentucky Derby, the odds opened 25-1 against him. But on May 7, 1925, he won the race as predicted, and became Oklahoma's first blue ribbon winner, Black Gold.

They called it the Bunion Derby and it was aptly named. The race was staged in 1928 to commemorate the opening of U.S. Route 66. One hundred and ninety-nine contestants entered the derby at Los Angeles to run 3,422.3 miles across country to New York. Andy Payne, a 19-year-old Cherokee from Foyil, covered the distance in 86 days, running an average of six miles an hour, to capture the first prize of $25,000. When young, he often ran to school instead of riding a horse like his brothers and sisters, thus developing his athletic ability.

Prentice Gautt, a black football player, had led Oklahoma City's Douglass High School football team to 76 straight victories in the state's segregated league. During the summer of 1956, OU coach Bud Wilkinson wanted him badly. But many influential supporters of the OU Sooners were opposed to a black player on the team. Finally, Wilkinson struck a bargain. Gautt would be allowed to try out for the team, if he made it, he would be given a scholarship. Gautt succeeded as Wilkinson knew he would, and became the first black player on the Sooner team.

The Hominy Indians were one of the first great professional football teams. Organized in 1924 in Oklahoma, they were soon winning so consistently they expanded their schedule coast to coast. On December 26, 1927, they beat the New York Giants, the newly crowned champions of the National Football League. For two years, the Hominy Indians remained unbeaten. Some businessmen talked of obtaining an NFL franchise in Tulsa for the team, but then came the Depression and the team disbanded after the 1932 season. All Indian players, they represented 11 tribes.

One of OU's most famous mascots was Mex, a mongrel dog. Mott Keyes, of Hollis, had found the dog in the fall of 1914 when he was serving in an Oklahoma field hospital on the Mexican border. When Keyes enrolled at OU in 1919, he brought Mex along. Mex quickly became the mascot of the Kappa Sigma fraternity and of the football team. Honorary memberships were heaped upon him, and he had his own OU sweater. When he died on April 30, 1928, his body was embalmed and the whole school turned out for his funeral. He was buried in a grave north of the stadium.

November 16, 1957, will long be remembered in Oklahoma as "Black Saturday." The OU Sooners had won 47 football games straight, setting a national record. On this day they had gone into the game an 18-point favorite. The 68,800 fans braving the cold in Norman believed the Sooners were unbeatable. The score remained tied until near the end of the game. Then with three minutes and fifty seconds left, the other team scored and OU's final pass in the end zone was intercepted. The crowd sat stunned, unable to believe OU had been beaten 7-0 by Notre Dame.

It is a tremendous job. Following each home football game at OU, fans leave an estimated six and a half tons of trash in Owen Stadium. In the past, it took university personnel a week to clean up the debris. Then in 1971 a new army of workers took over the chore. Today, they still carry on, an industrious group of 165 men, women, and children, who begin work as soon as the game is over. Their task is usually finished by 10 p.m., for which they are paid $5,000. They are members of the Norman Church of Jesus Christ of Latter Day Saints.

Whatever happened to the old polo field on the OU campus? It is doing well, thank you, on a golf course in northwestern Oklahoma. In 1979, a committee for the golf course purchased all the grass on the polo field and trucked it to its new location. It took 22 round trips of 150 miles each to haul all the sod. The golf course is situated in a wooded area in the sand hills of the North Canadian River. Those playing the 18-hole course are apt to see deer, wild turkey, and buffalo at Boiling Springs State Park near Woodward.

PART 5. OKLAHOMA ODDITIES

MATTERS OF STATE

Oklahoma has its share of state symbols.

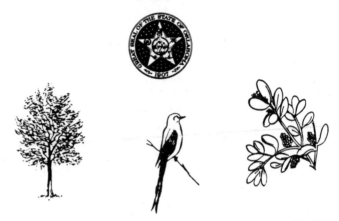

How did we get the name of our state? After the Civil War the Five Civilized tribes ceded the western half of Indian Territory to the federal government on which to settle other tribes. Delegates to the Choctaw-Chickasaw Treaty in Washington drew up a plan for an intertribal council to govern the proposed state. When the question arose as to the governor's title, Reverand Allen Wright, a Choctaw delegate said, "We will call him 'governor of *Okla homa,*'"meaning "Red People" in the Choctaw language. No Indian state was ever formed but the name remained.

It may not look impressive but it is the most important point in Oklahoma. It is located by a nondescript 54 x 18-inch slab of sandstone, in a pasture about six miles west of Davis. In 1870, surveyors, while preparing the land for settlement, set the sandstone marker upright in a pile of stones. They carved the letters "I.P." on three sides of the stone. It marks the intersection of the Base Line and Indian Meridian. It is from here, the Initial Point, that all lands in Oklahoma, except the Panhandle, receive their legal descriptions.

Our Oklahoma constitution is the longest in the nation. During ratification in 1907 it took 18 hours to read it. Those signing it hailed from 17 states and 2 foreign countries. The oldest signer was Clem Rogers, the father of Will Rogers, and the youngest was William C. Liedtke, 24, from Eufaula. Among the signers were 47 farmers, 27 lawyers, 12 merchants, 3 newspaper men, 3 teachers, 6 preachers, 2 doctors, 2 investors, a civil engineer, a bookkeeper, a miners' union official, and a student. It was truly a document of the people.

The first signature on Oklahoma's lengthy constitution was signed by not one, but two pens. The first pen was most unusual, signifying the blending of two cultures, that of the red man and the white man. It was a quill pen, made from the feather of an eagle captured in Kay County and a stem of alfalfa from the farm of "Alfalfa Bill" Murray, chairman of the constitutional convention. Murray wrote "Wm. H." with the quill pen then finished his signature with a special pen given for the occasion by William Jennings Bryan.

It was a grand occasion. Following the presidential proclamation, on Statehood Day, November 16, 1907, Oklahoma citizens staged a symbolic wedding between Indian Territory and Oklahoma Territory. The event was held at the Carnegie Library in Guthrie before a crowd of 20,000 people. Representing Oklahoma Territory as the groom was C. G. "Gristmill" Jones of Oklahoma City, who had built the first flour mill in the territory. Mrs. Anna Trainor Bennett, a native born one-sixteenth Cherokee from Muskogee was chosen as the bride.

On June 16, 1908, 92 women met in Guthrie to carry out a special project. Federal law stated that no national flag carrying the 46th star could be officially flown until July 4 after the state's admission to the union. The Philadelphia Betsy Ross Association had asked the Oklahoma women to make a flag for this purpose. The flag was completed in one day, then taken to

Philadelphia and flown over Independence Hall all afternoon. Returned to the state, the flag was given to the *U.S.S. Oklahoma*, and was on the ship when it was bombed and capsized at Pearl Harbor, December 7, 1941.

The term "Old Sunnybrook" often drew a smile from early Oklahoma politicians. During the first legislature in 1908, in spite of the state's prohibition ordinance, Speaker William Murray waged a vigorous fight for a state dispensary system, making beer, wine, and whiskey available for medicinal purposes. Murray insisted no law abiding man ought to have to violate the law when the need arose. Finally, the amendment was accepted and the dispensary system went into operation. Selling for 80 cents a pint, the state's official brand name was Sunnybrook.

The mistletoe, a parasite with waxy leaves and almost indiscernable blossoms, seemed a strange thing to select as a state emblem. It had been associated with the Celtic Druids. But those who defended it said it had been a delight to the 89ers, in full bloom that first Christmas. Housewives decorated their crude homes with it, and placed it on lonely graves that winter. First chosen to represent Oklahoma Territory at Chicago's Columbian Exposition in 1893, the mistletoe officially became our state flower in 1910.

The soldiers at Fort Sill said they wouldn't carry our first state flag, lest they be mistaken for the Russian Army. Citizens didn't like hanging the flag on their porches for fear neighbors would think they had scarlet fever. The banner had a red field with a white star edged in blue, and the number "46" centered on the star. Many people didn't even know Oklahoma had a state flag. We didn't, our first four years as a state. Then Mrs. W. R. Clement, Stillwater, decided things were amiss and designed this first flag which was adopted in 1911 with little opposition.

Strangely enough, the Oklahoma state directory carried a picture of a dome on the capitol from 1917 to 1930. But truth is Oklahoma is one of seven states in the nation that has never had a dome. That was not the way capitol architects planned it. Original blueprints called for a dome, and in addition, a series of Parisian arches on South Lincoln Boulevard to line the approach to the capitol. But lack of funds put an end to their dreams when the capitol building was finished in 1917. Since then all appropriations for a dome have been voted down.

Oklahoma's second state flag created considerable suspicion. The Catholics asked if the crosses on it represented the Klu Klux Klan; the Klu Klux Klan asked if they represented the Catholics. The flag was adopted in 1925 following a statewide contest. The winning banner featured an Osage warrior's shield against a field of blue, with pendant eagle feathers, a peace pipe, and an olive branch. The questionable row of crosses, signifying stars, were simply part of the decoration on the original shield from which designer Louise Fluke drew her model.

When bird lovers nominated the fiesty scissor-tail as the official symbol of Oklahoma, law makers laughed. But the birders' persistence paid off and on Bird Day, May 1, 1951, this bird, with a tail twice as long as its body, became our official mascot. Rivaling tropical birds in its coloring and unusual plummage, its feathers are used in ceremonies in the Native American Church. Protected by the Migratory Bird Act, the bird is found mainly in Texas, Kansas, and Oklahoma, with Oklahoma being the principal breeding ground.

Richard Rodgers and Oscar Hammerstein, creators of Oklahoma's state song, had never visited Oklahoma, nor did they know what Southwestern music sounded like. Hammerstein simply looked out the window at his Pennsylvania farm and tried to envision Oklahoma corn, and wrote "Oh, what a beautiful morning!" Rodgers then set the words to music. Nevertheless, Oklahomans took the song to heart during the 1946 state premier. With a push in 1953 by a young legislator from McAlester, George Nigh, "Oklahoma!" replaced our first state song, "Oklahoma — A Toast."

In 1968, the Oklahoma legislature adopted the Rose Rock as the official state rock. It is found in only a few places in the world, including a narrow band in central Oklahoma. Deposited 250 million years ago, the Rose Rocks are barite crystals formed in petal-like clusters. When the Cherokee Indians first saw them, the Rose Rocks inspired a legend. Hundred of people had died on the Trail of Tears. The Cherokees said God decided to commemorate their courage. He turned their drops into of blood and tears into the shape of a Cherokee Rose, a symbol of their home state, Georgia.

The buffalo was a walking supermarket, providing almost everything the Plains Indian needed including bones for war clubs, hide for tipis, clothing, and robes. His meat was cut and dried for future use. His tail made a fly swatter, his horns became spoons and ladles, and from his hooves came glue. His sinews provided bow strings and lacing. The Indians braided his hair into halters and ropes. At one time more than 50 million buffalo grazed the plains. When they vanished a way of life vanished with them. The buffalo became our state animal in 1972.

Oklahoma not only has an official state flower but an official state wildflower as well. The *Garillardia puchella*, or Indian Blanket, was adopted by the state legislature on March 20, 1986. Daisy-like with red petals tipped in yellow, the Indian Blanket brightens the Oklahoma countryside from May through September. It was recommended as our state wildflower by botanist Dr. Doyle McCoy, who had long felt our highways needed some kind of floral decoration. The Indian Blanket was suitable, growing in a wide variety of soils.

WONDERS OF NATURE

Oklahoma has a wide variety of natural attractions.

The Arbuckle Mountains once stood higher than the Rocky Mountains. Created in the late Pennsylvania age, they have been reduced to their present height by ground movement and erosion. Among the strangest features of the mountain range are long rows of rock which march across the hillsides as precisely as well ordered rows of tombstones. These are the result of layers of the earth being tilted on their sides in eons past. A five mile hike across these layers can carry one across 400,000,000 years of geologic time.

Oklahoma's famed red earth covers two-thirds of the state and occurs predominately in three distinct regions in western Oklahoma, central Oklahoma, and in the Cross Timbers. The soil obtains its distinctive color from hematite, an iron oxide compound. It was formed 250 million years ago during the Permian geological age from sedimentary rocks when the area was covered by water. Today, this red earth provides the basis of our cattle, oil, brick, and pottery industries. It also gives us some of our most intriguing sculptures when eroded by wind and water.

Cimarron County in the Panhandle was identified as the center of the Dust Bowl during the 1930s. Oddly enough, during the same period WPA workers began excavating a dinosaur graveyard in the area. They also found petrified logs six-feet in diameter. These fossils told of the Mesozoic past, when vast inland seas flowed here. Giant turtles and plesiosaurs swam in the warm swamps among the tropical trees and ferns. Enormous reptiles lumbered about for more than 100 million years. Then abruptly it all vanished as the earth became colder and drier.

The largest chunk of the world's oldest petrified tree now reposes at East Central University at Ada. Pigs rooted up the fragments, believed to be about 250 millions years old, in 1913. The Chickasaw owner told local geologist John Fitts of the find, who in turn notified Dr. David White of the U.S. Geglogical Survey in Washington, D.C., of the discovery. White set out to transfer the remains to the Smithsonian Institution, but died before he could accomplish this. In 1936, Fitts gave the fragments to ECU, which glued them back together.

Woodward County's Alabaster Caverns are the largest of their kind in the world. This fairyland of pink and white alabaster tunnels beneath the earth for more than a half-mile. It took nature more than 200 million years to create the caverns. They provide a home for seven species of bats and a rare blind fish. Through the years a succession of Indians, cowboys, and homesteaders have visited here. Early settlers hauled tons of guano from the caverns for use as fertilizer. Located south of Freedom, the caverns were purchased as a state park in 1953.

Our state's tallest tree is located on Persimmon Creek, four miles southeast of Woodward. A cottonwood, it is estimated to be 130 years old, and is 78 feet tall, and 28 feet four inches in diameter, according to the state forestry divison.

The previous champion was a bald cypress located in McCurtain County, which was estimated to be 2,000 years old. That tree stood 118 feet tall and measured 32 feet four inches around. The owner claimed approximately 10,000 persons visited the tree each year before it was killed by lightning in 1983.

Indians called the salt plains The Great Nescutanga. George Sibley was the first white man to visit here in 1811. He stared in wonder at the vast sheet of crystalized salt which spread over the land along the Cimarron River in northwestern Oklahoma. In places, the water boiled up as clear as crystal through the thick rock crust. But even before the Louisiana Purchase, President Thomas Jefferson had heard of the salt plain and thought it had great production potential. It was not until 1920, though, that Ezra Blackmon set up a small harvesting plant here, which is still in operation.

Oklahoma is not known for its earthquakes, yet more than 65 have rocked the state since 1811. In 1904, one tremor left a gash three miles long in the earth near Capron. But the most active region is in the Oklahoma City-El Reno region, in what is called the Nemaha ridge system, a buried mountain complex extending from the Arbuckles to Omaha, Nebraska. Oklahoma's worst quake was centered here, five miles south of Oklahoma City, on April 9, 1952. It was felt all over the state, registered 5.5 on the Ricter scale, and rocked buildings in Oklahoma City for 23 minutes.

"Rock Mary," near present Hinton, was the most prominent landmark on the California Road. It was first seen by Captain Randolph B. Marcy's expedition on May 23, 1894. Marcy was escorting an emigrant party of 500 to the California gold fields. Two young officers, Lieutenants J. H. Simpson and M. P. Harrison (brother of President Benjamin Harrison) were courting the favor of a young belle in the party. Racing to the crest of the landmark, they planted an American flag and named the landmark in honor of Mary Conway, cousin of President James Madison.

Prior to settlement, a virtually impenetrable forest extended in a belt 5 to 30 miles wide through central Oklahoma. Washington Irving likened the phenomenon in 1832 to "struggling through forests of cast iron." The brushy section created a natural boundary between the hardwoods of the eastern forests and the western grasslands. It was so striking it inspired a legend that it had been planted by an ancient lost race of Mound Builders to mark their western boundary. Today, little remains of this once extensive forest, the Cross Timbers.

At one time the passenger pigeon darkened the skies of Indian Territory by the millions. The birds perched in trees so thickly they broke the branches. Then hunters began to trap them and ship them back east by the barrelful. The birds began to disappear. Before the close of the 1890s, they were becoming scarce; a few more years and they were gone. The Cherokees believed the birds had attempted to cross the ocean, or were caught in a tornado, because they left one day and never came back. The passenger pigeon is now extinct.

The common cattail is one of the most versatile plants to be found in Oklahoma. Camp cooks can add its pollen to biscuits to obtain a golden color and impart a corn flavor. Or the male blossom can be boiled before it pollinates and it tastes like corn. The roots can be ground into flour, and the rushes woven into baskets. The stem makes a natural polishing agent for scouring blackened pots. Early Indian mothers used the plant's bouyant fuzz as "diapers" for their infants, and the U.S. Navy filled lifejackets with the fuzz during World War II.

The armadillo has been termed a "Hoover Hog," and a poor man's pig. Prior to 1936, these hard-shelled little animals were not seen in Oklahoma. Then these short-legged creatures, which the Aztecs called *Aztochtli*, meaning "tortoise-rabbit," drifted into the southern part of Oklahoma from Texas. Since then they have been seen in 12 other states. When in danger, these comical looking animals jump straight up three or four feet, their fear response. While they're cute, it is best advised to leave them alone, for they can also transmit leprosy.

In 1930, officials discovered a 590 pound meteorite laying in a gully at Lake Murray State Park. Not knowing what else to do with it, they left it there for 37 years, wasting away. Then came the space age and scientists took a new interest in the meteorite. They sawed a slice from the ultra hard piece of metal, which took them 321 hours, using silicon carbine blades and carborundum. They determined the watermelon sized object was an extremely rare specimen of meteoritic nickeliferous iron, Today, the meteor is on display in Tucker Tower.

On April 9, 1947, Oklahoma's worst tornado roared out of the Texas Panhandle near Arnett, and left the state near Alva. Two miles wide, it killed 185 people in a three-state area, injured 1,000, and destroyed more than $1 million worth of property. In Woodward alone, the storm killed 105 people and injured 720. With winds clocked at over 200 miles per hour, the storm never left the ground during the course of its 221 mile path of destruction. It still ranks among the top ten tornados of all time.

MAN-MADE ATTRACTIONS

Oklahoma's tourist attractions range from the usual to the unusual.

In 1884, Comanche chief Quannah Parker built a 12-room mansion near Cache. One day Quannah was visiting on the porch with two Texans when a star-studded military vehicle stopped in front. The rather pompous officer greeted Quannah and asked permission to cross his land on military maneuvers. Later the owner asked the Texans what all the stars on the vehicle meant. He was told they indicated the officer was the leader of many warriors. Quannah stated he was too, and shortly after, 14 white stars adorned the roof of his home, now called the Star House.

The Scottish Rite Cathedral in Guthrie is the largest building of its kind in the world. It seats 3,500 people, contains an organ of 5,280 pipes, and has a massive stage with 118 backdrops and lighting switchboard. It was built during Oklahoma's territorial days on a ten-acre park near the eastern edge of the town. Plans were to build the state capitol on the site. A building was erected here called Convention Hall, which is now incorporated as the east section of this massive structure, but mainly the building is known for its service to Masonry.

The Round Barn of Arcadia was one of the most famous landmarks on Route 66 in Oklahoma. William Harrison "Big Bill" Odor built the barn on his homestead in 1898. Unorthodox in shape, it took six months to complete the structure which stood 60 feet in diameter and 43 feet in height. All of the lumber came from his farm. To shape the rafters, Odor soaked green burr-oak timber in water until it became soft enough to bend in a specially made form. Today, the landmark still stands but in July 1988 the roof caved in. It has since been rebuilt.

One of Guthrie's most famous buildings may well have been a two-story privy in the town's commercial district. Built of brick, the 8 x 10 foot privy was located behind the Triumph Building on lot 23. Nathaniel McKay, a transplanted easterner turned Guthrie developer, was granted a deed to build the privy on July 28, 1899. The city council charged him with maintaining the privy and keeping it in good repair. A covered walkway assured the tenants access from the second floor of the Triumph Building, and of two seats on each floor in the privy.

Located 14 miles west of Bartlesville, Woolaroc is best known for its Indian and early west museum, but in the beginning it was the private estate of oil baron Frank Phillips. Thousands of people visited here during the early 1920s and he frequently threw open the gates for company picnics and other gatherings. The unusual name was taken from the woods, lakes, and rocks that dominated the rugged 17,000 acre tract. Phillips built the lodge at Woolaroc in 1926, and whenever he was at the ranch, a special flag was flown before the building, indicating his presence.

The statue of Oklahoma's "Pioneer Woman" was dedicated at Ponca City on April 22, 1930. In the beginning, there were 12 models, created by the world's best sculptors. They had been commissioned in 1927 by E. W. Marland as a tribute to "all women of the sunbonnet everywhere." The finished models were sent on a national tour and the public voted on its choice. The art critics disagreed with the public's selection, but Marland agreed with it, and Brooklyn sculptor Bryant Baker was commissioned to create the final 17-foot statue for $250,000.

Oklahoma's Pensacola Dam cost $20 million and was the biggest construction job the state had ever seen. Daming up the Grand River was first conceived as a private project in the 1890s, but it wasn't until 1935 that the Oklahoma legislature created the Grand River Dam Authority. Thousands of men worked on the project, clearing 20,000 acres of timber, and laying down 28,000 carloads of cement and steel. When finished, it stood ten stories high, the longest multiple-arch dam in the world. It now provides electrical power for 18 counties.

Tucker Tower is Lake Murray's most famous landmark. The tall, rock building stands like a fortress on a cliff 25 feet above the water. Construction began on the building in 1934 and work continued intermittently until 1947. Originally, the tower-like structure was designed as headquarters for the U.S. Forest Service. Later, plans called for it to become the governor's summer mansion. But Tucker Tower was never used for either purpose. It remained useless until 1950 when it was converted into a geological museum.

"Showmen's Rest" in Hugo's Mount Olivet Cemetery, is the largest cemetery of its kind in the world, and the most unusual in Oklahoma. While other cemeteries are dignified and somber looking, this one exhibits a spirit of fun. Here one can find a tombstone shaped like a tent or a ticket booth, and see dancing elephants. More elephant trainers are buried here than any other place in the world. Other circus occupations are equally well represented here, as are the top names in the circus world. Established in 1961, the cemetery is a tribute to the Big Top.

It couldn't be done, stated the U.S. Corps of Engineers. What they were referring to was a proposed project for building a reservoir near Norman on the Little River. There just wasn't enough water out there to fill it, they said. So Norman joined Del City and Midwest City to form the Central

Oklahoma Water Users Association, and captured the interest of the Bureau of Reclamation. Today, Lake Thunderbird, which was dedicated on October 14, 1965, covers more than 6,000 acres, and is one of the most heavily used recreation areas in the state.

The Arkansas-Verdigris Navigation System and Port Catoosa in eastern Oklahoma was one of the most challenging and complex engineering feats of its kind in history. It took more than 20 years to plan and build, and cost $1.2 billion, four times that of the Panama Canal. When the waterway was officially opened on December 31, 1968, it bacame the nation's northernmost, year-round, ice-free seaport, bringing the ocean to Oklahoma. Today the 436 mile navigation system transports an estimated 2.5 million tons of freight annually.

The *U.S.S. Batfish*, Oklahoma's only submarine, holds the record for sinking the most enemy subs in a single patrol during World War I, three of them within 72 hours. The *Batfish* is now docked at Muskogee's War Memorial Park, which was formally dedicated on Memorial Day, 1973. The vessel is 323 feet long, with 18,000 tons of displacement. It took two boats and six flotilla barges to bring the submarine through 15 locks of the McClelland-Kerr Navigation System from Port Orange, Texas, to Muskogee, a distance of 1,350 miles.

One day Cedar Lake was there and the next it wasn't. The 600 stockholders of the private housing community had built the lake in a spring-fed canyon ten miles north of Cogar in Canadian County. The lake covered 75 acres. Then on November 7, 1986, the lake began to disappear. The water drained through a fissure in the lake bottom, traveled a half-mile underground and erupted through the side of a hill. A county road was closed and two homes were evacuated for a time. Within 37 hours the water was all gone, leaving the residents staring at the muddy lake bottom.

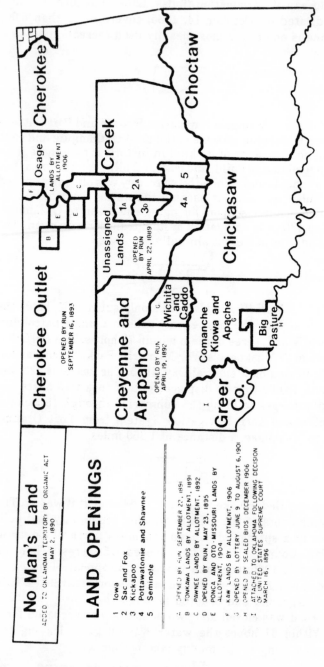

No Man's Land

ADDED TO OKLAHOMA TERRITORY BY ORGANIC ACT
MAY 2, 1890

Cherokee

Cherokee Outlet

OPENED BY RUN
SEPTEMBER 16, 1893

Osage

LANDS BY
ALLOTMENT
1906

F

B

E

E

C

Creek

Choctaw

Unassigned
Lands

OPENED
BY RUN
APRIL 22, 1889

1A

2A

3D

4A

5

Chickasaw

Cheyenne and
Arapaho

OPENED BY RUN,
APRIL 19, 1892

Wichita
and
Caddo

G

Comanche
Kiowa and
Apache

Big
Pasture

H

Greer
Co.

I

LAND OPENINGS

1 Iowa
2 Sac and Fox
3 Kickapoo
4 Pottawatomie and Shawnee
5 Seminole

A OPENED BY RUN SEPTEMBER 22, 1891
B TONKAWA LANDS BY ALLOTMENT, 1891
C PAWNEE LANDS BY ALLOTMENT, 1892
D OPENED BY RUN, MAY 23, 1895
E PONCA AND OTO-MISSOURI LANDS BY
   ALLOTMENT, 1904
F KAW LANDS BY ALLOTMENT, 1906
G OPENED BY LOTTERY JUNE 9 TO AUGUST 6, 1901
H OPENED BY SEALED BIDS DECEMBER 1906
I ATTACHED TO OKLAHOMA FOLLOWING DECISION
   OF UNITED STATES SUPREME COURT
   MARCH 16, 1896

OKLAHOMA LAND OPENINGS

LAND OPENING	DATE
Unassigned Lands	April 22, 1889
No Man's Land	May 2, 1890
Sac & Fox, Potawatomi, Iowa, Shawnee	September 22, 1891
Tonkawa	October 21, 1891
Cheyenne, Arapaho	April 19, 1892
Cherokee Outlet, Peoria, Pawnee, Tonkawa	September 16, 1893
Greer County	March 16, 1896
Kickapoo	April 23, 1897
Choctaw, Chickasaw, Seminole	December 16, 1897
Wichita & Caddo, Comanche, Apache	June 9 to August 6, 1901
Creek	June 25, 1901
Kaw	February 1, 1902
Osage	June 26, 1906
Big Pasture	December 17, 1906

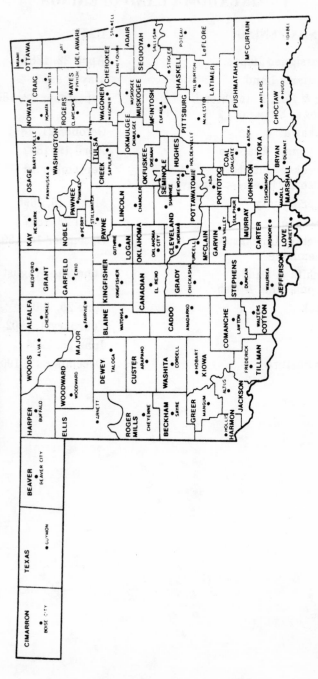

OKLAHOMA COUNTIES

FAMOUS PEOPLE FROM OKLAHOMA

Many famous people have lived in Oklahoma. Some were born here; others lived here at one time or do so now. All contributed to the development of the state. The towns and cities these people once called home follow each name. This list has been updated and expanded from an earlier edition of this book.

Name	Achivement/Occupation	Town
Troy Aikman	Football	Henryetta
Carl Albert	Speaker, U.S. House of Representatives	McAlester
Joseph A. Albertson	Founder, supermarket chain	Yukon
Gene Autry	Actor, Musician	Gene Autry, Sapulpa
Hoyt Axton	Musician	Duncan, Tulsa
Lou Ballard	Composer	Miami, Tulsa
Russell Bates	Author	Anadarko
Black Beaver	Indian Scout	Anadarko
Johnny Bench	Baseball	Binger, Oklahoma City
John Berryman	Poet, Pulitzer Prize	Anadarko, McAlester
Jack Bickham	Author	Norman
Dennis Byrd	Football	Mustang
Baxter Black	Cowboy poet, humorist	Noble
Don Blanding	Poet	Kingfisher
David Boren	Govenor, legislator, OU president	Seminole, Norman
William "Hopalong Cassidy" Boyd	Actor	Tulsa
Paul & Thomas Braniff	Aviation pioneers	Oklahoma City
Garth Brooks	Singer	Yukon
Allison Brown	Miss Teen U.S.A.	Edmond
Anita Bryant	Entertainer	Midwest City, Tulsa
Lon Chaney	Actor	Oklahoma City
Lon Chaney, Jr.	Actor	Oklahoma City
C.J. Cherryh	Author	Norman, Okla. City
Jesse Chisholm	Pioneer trader	Geary
Yvonne Chouteau	Ballerina	Norman, Vinita
Charles Christian	Musician	Oklahoma City
Roy Clark	Musician	Tulsa
Joseph "Jocko" Clark	U.S. Navy Admiral, WWII hero	Pryor

Jerrie Cobb	First woman astronaut	Norman, Okla. City
W. C. Coleman	Inventor, lamp and stove	Kingfisher
Nadia Comaneci	Olympic gymnast	Norman
Bart Conner	Olympic gymnast	Norman
Danny Cooksey	Actor	Midwest City
Gordon Cooper	Astronaut	Shawnee, Tecumseh
Joan Crawford	Actress	Lawton
Walter Cronkite	Broadcast journalist	Oklahoma City
Dan Dailey	Rodeo	Edmond
Bill Dalton	Outlaw	Ardmore, Ingalls
Alvin Dark	Baseball	Comanche
Gail Davies	Singer	Broken Bow
Steve Davis	Football, TV announcer	Sallisaw
Paul Dean	Baseball	Holdenville
Jerome "Dizzy" Dean	Baseball	Holdenville
Angie Debo	Historian, author	Marshall
John Denver	Musician	Corn, Clinton
Joe Diffie	Musician, singer	Alma
Robert Duncan	Author	Norman
Ronnie Dunn	Musician, singer	Tulsa
Candice Early	Actress	Lawton
Frank B. Eaton	Old West lawman	Perkins
Mr. Ed	"The Talking Horse"	Tahlequah
Ronnie Claire Edwards	Actress	Hugo
Douglas Edwards	Reporter	Ada
Blake Edwards	Film producer	Tulsa
Ralph Ellison	Author	Oklahoma City
Connie "Carol Finch" Fedderson	Author	Union City
Tom Ferguson	Rodeo	Miami
Charles "Pretty Boy" Floyd	Outlaw	Akins, Sallisaw
Jennie Flynn	First woman fighter pilot	Enid
Grant & Carolyn Foreman	Historians	Muskogee
Jay Fox	Director	Purcell
Kay Francis	Actress	Oklahoma City
John Hope Franklin	Black historian	Rentiesville
Lane Frost	World champion bull rider	Lane
James Garner	Actor	Norman
Owen K. Garriott	Astronaut	Enid
David Gates	Musician	Tulsa
Edward L. Gaylord	Newspaper publisher, owner Grand Old Opry	Oklahoma City
Frank Geer	Newspaper editor	Guthrie
Geronimo	Apache warrior	Apache, Fort Sill, Lawton
Father Gregory Gerrer	Artist	El Reno, Shawnee
J. Paul Getty	Financier	Tulsa

Name	Occupation	Location
Alice Ghostley	Actress	Henryetta, Norman
Vince Gill	Musician, singer	Norman, Okla. City
Jack Ging	Actor	Alva, Norman
S. N. Goldman	Inventor of shopping cart	Ardmore, Oklahoma City
Chester Gould	Cartoonist	Pawnee
Curt Gowdy	Sports reporter	Oklahoma City
Clu Gulager	Actor	Tahlequah, Muskogee
Woody Guthrie	Singer/Songwriter	Okemah
Jean Hager	Author	Tulsa
Rosa Lee "Aunt Jemima" Hall	Advertising	Oklahoma City
Argus Hamilton	Comedian, columnist	Poteau, Oklahoma City, Enid
Carol Hamilton	Poet laureate, author	Midwest City
Mary Hart	TV anchorwoman	Oklahoma City
Jim Hartz	TV new reporter	Tulsa
Paul Harvey	Broadcast journalist	Tulsa
Van Heflin	Actor	Oklahoma City
Bill Scott (Weldon Hill)	Author	Purcell, Skeedee
Tony Hillerman	Author	Sacred Heart
Stanley Hoig	Author	Gage, Edmond
Allan Houser	Sculptor, stone carver	Apache
Temple Houston	Attorney	Woodward
Sam Houston	President, Texas Republic	Fort Gibson
Ron Howard	Actor/Director	Duncan
Carl Hubbell	Baseball	Meeker
Patrick J. Hurley	Statesman	Tulsa
Henry P. Iba	Basketball	Stillwater
Wanda Jackson	Musician	Oklahoma City
Marquis James	Author	Enid
Jane Jayroe	Miss America, 1967	Clinton, Laverne, Oklahoma City
Ben Johnson	Actor	Pawhuska
Jimmy Johnson	Football coach, commentator	Stillwater, Norman
Larry Jones	Evangelist, Feed the Children	Oklahoma City
Jennifer Jones	Actress	Oklahoma City
Frank Keating	Govenor, legislator	Oklahoma City
Toby Keith	Singer	Moore
Maybelle Kennedy	U. S. Treasurer	Pawhuska
Robert S. Kerr	Oilman, senator	Ada, Oklahoma City, Poteau
Barney Kessel	Musician	Muskogee
Black Kettle	Cheyenne Chief	Cheyenne
R.A. Lafferty	Author	Tulsa
Gordon William "Pawnee Bill" Lillie	Wild West Show	Pawnee

Clevon Little	Actor	Chickasha
Nancy Lopez-Knight	Golf	Tulsa
Shannon Lucid	Astronaut	Oklahoma City, Bethany
Clara Luper	Civil rights activist	Oklahoma City
Louis L'Amour	Author	Oklahoma City
Wilma Mankiller	Chief, Cherokee Nation	Tahlequah
Mickey Mantle	Baseball	Commerce
E. W. Marland	Oilman	Ponca City
John "Pepper" Martin	Baseball	Temple, Oklahoma City
Curtis Ann Matlock	Author	Minco
Leon McAuliffe	Musician	Tulsa
Rue McClanahan	Actress	Duncan
Reba McEntire	Singer, Musician	Chockie, Durant, Stringtown
Dean McGee	Oilman	Oklahoma City
Carol McGee	Newsman, inventor of parking meter	Oklahoma City, Tulsa
Frank McGee	Broadcast journalist	Oklahoma City
Jay McShann	Jazz pianist	Muskogee
Clem McSpadden	Pro rodeo announcer	Chelsea
Perle Mesta	Washington, D.C. hostess	Oklahoma City
Augusta Metcalfe	Artist	Durham
Vera Miles	Actress	Boise City
Joe Miller	101 Ranch Wild West Show	Lamont
Roger Miller	Musician	Erick
Zack Miller	101 Ranch Wild West Show	Lamont
Jody Miller	Singer	Blanchard
Shannon Miller	Olympic gymnast	Edmond
George W. Miller	Founder, 101 Ranch	Lamont
Dale Mitchell	Baseball	Cloud Chief
Tom Mix	Cowboy, Actor	Dewey, Guthrie
Al Momaday	Indian artist	Mountain View
N. Scott Momaday	Author	Lawton
Gil Morgan	Golf	Weowka
Bill Moyers	Journalist, statesman	Hugo
Zack Mulhall	WildWest Show	Mulhall
Lucille Mulhall	First show cowgirl	Mulhall
Bobby Murcer	Baseball	Oklahoma City
Lynne Murphy	Author	Edmond
William "Alfalfa Bill" Murray	Politician	Tishomingo
Russell Myers	Cartoonist	Tulsa
Carrie Nation	Prohibitionist	Guthrie, Seiling
The Nixons	Music	Norman
Chuck Norris	Actor	Wilson
Steve Nunno	Gymnastic coach	Edmond

Joseph Oklahombi	World War I Hero	Wright City
Sarah Orwig	Author	Oklahoma City
A. Y. Owen	Photographer	Cheyenne, Oklahoma City
Steve Owens	Football	Miami, Norman
Patti Page	Musician	Claremore, Tulsa
Clarence Page	Aviator	Oklahoma City
John L. Peters	Founder, World Neighbors	Oklahoma City
Frank & Waite Phillips	Oilmen	Bartlesville, Tulsa
Bill Pickett	Inventor, bulldogging	Ponca City
Brad Pitt	Actor	Shawnee
Mary Kay Place	Actress	Tulsa
William Reid Pogue	Astronaut	Okemah
Darrell Porter	Baseball	Oklahoma City
Wiley Post	Aviator	Maysville
Susan Powell	Miss America, 1981	Elk City
Paula Prentiss	Entertainer	Tulsa
Tony Randall	Actor	Tulsa
Deborah A. "Arlene James" Rather	Author	Duncan
Donna Reed	Actress	Tulsa
Allie Reynolds	Baseball	Bethany, Stillwater
Paul Richard	Baseball	Muskogee
Lynn Riggs	Author	Claremore
Oral Roberts	Evangelist	Tulsa
Dennis Rodman	Basketball	Weatherford
Alice Mary Robertson	First U.S. Congresswoman, Founder, Tulsa University	Muskogee
Dale Robertson	Actor	Oklahoma City
Will Rogers	Humorist/entertainer	Claremore, Oologah
Stuart Roosa	Astronaut, Apollo 14	Claremore
Dan Rowan	Comedian	Beggs
Darrell Royal	Football	Hollis
Jimmy Rushing	Musician, blues singer	Oklahoma City
Leon Russell	Musician	Tulsa
Will Sampson	Artist, actor	Okmulgee
Barry Sanders	Football	Stillwater
Gaylord Sartain	Actor	Tulsa
Sequoyah	Inventor, Cheokee alphabet	Sallisaw
Jim Shoulders	World champion cowboy	Henryetta
Billy Simms	Football	Norman
Ada Sipuel-Fisher	Black activist, OU regent	Langston, Norman
William Skelly	Oilman	Tulsa
Norma Smallwood	Miss America, 1926	Tulsa
Shawntel Smith	Miss America, 1996	Muldrow
Warren Spahn	Baseball	Hartshorne
Thomas P. Stafford	Astronaut	Oklahoma City

John Starks	NBA All-Star	Tulsa
Kay Starr	Musician	Dougherty
Belle Starr	Outlaw	Eufaula
Dora Stohl	Actress	Oklahoma City
Willard Stone	Sculptor	Locust Grove
Wes Studi	Actor	Tahlequah
George M. Stutton	Artist	Norman
Dwight Swain	Author	Norman
Barry Switzer	Football	Norman
Maria Tallchief	Ballerina	Fairfax
Majorie Tallchief	Ballerina	Fairfax
Henry "Heck" Thomas	Lawman	Lawton, Guthrie
Hank Thompson	Musician	Sand Springs
Jim Thorpe	Athlete	Yale
Jerome Tiger	Indian artist	Muskogee
Johnny Tiger	Indian artist	Eufaula, Muskogee
Bill Tilghman	Lawman	Chandler, Cromwell
Clarence Tinker	U.S. Army general, aviator	Pawhuska
Truman "Pinky" Tomlin	Actor, musician	Durant, Norman
The Tractors	Music	Tulsa
Billy Tubbs	Basketball coach	Norman
Conway Twitty	Musician	Oklahoma City, Norman
Billy Vessels	Football	Cleveland, Norman
Jimmy Wakely	Musician	Oklahoma City
Judith Wall	Author	Norman
Karen Wallace	Miss Black America, 1996	Oklahoma City
Sam Walton	Wal-Mart founder	Kingfisher
Paul Waner	Baseball	Harrah
Lloyd Waner	Baseball	Harrah
J. C. Watts	Football, legislator	Checotah, Norman
Dennis Weaver	Actor	Norman
Jimmy Webb	Musician	Elk City
Bryan White	Singer	Oklahoma City
Bud Wilkinson	Football	Norman
J. R. Williams	Actor	Stigler
Mason Williams	Musician	Oklahoma City
Johnnie Lee Wills	Musician	Tulsa
Bob Wills	Musician	Tulsa
Charles Banks Wilson	Artist	Miami
Shelby "Sheb" Wooley	Actor/musician	Plainview
Gretchen Wyler	Actress	Bartlesville
Raymond A. Young	TG&Y chairman	Kingfisher

OTHER FACTS ABOUT OKLAHOMA

Oklahoma ranks first in a number of things. The following list was compiled by the Oklahoma Department of Commerce.

- Oklahoma had the first flowing commercial oil well in the world.

- Oklahoma had the first Boy Scout Troup in America, 1909.

- Oklahoma has more shoreline than the Atlantic and Gulf Coast combined.

- Twenty-three per cent of the state, slightly more than 10 million acres, is covered by forests with 141 tree varieties.

- Oklahoma has approximately 44 acres of land to every acre of water.

- Oklahoma's average temperature is 60.5 degrees; average rainfall for the state is 33.39 inches.

- Oklahoma averages 350 "flying" days per year with little fog or smog.

- The largest field of holly in the United States is found in Oklahoma's McCurtain County.

- American Airlines had its beginning in Oklahoma.

- Two brothers from Oklahoma began the Cessna Corporation.

- The first passenger plane was built in Oklahoma.

- Carry Nation lived and published her temperance newspaper in Guthrie.

- Buck Jones, movie actor and son of a Perry rancher, lost his life saving lives at the Cocoanut Grove fire in Boston in 1942.

- The 45th "Thunderbird" Division, which achieved a record of valor and heroism during World War II, originated in Oklahoma.

- The world's largest air material center is Tinker Air Force Base in Midwest City.

- Oklahoma is home of the National Cowboy Hall of Fame and Western Heritage Center, located in Oklahoma City.

- The University of Oklahoma football team has won the National Championship six times.

- OU's Pride of Oklahoma was named the No. 1 collegiate marching band in the nation in 1987.

- OSU ranks No. 1 in collegiate baseball and golf teams.

- The No. 1 American art collection is located at Gilcrease Museum, Tulsa.

- Oklahoma has the No. 1 rated Vocational-Technical School system.

- The University of Tulsa ranks No. 1 in research on the life and work of author James Joyce.

- The largest McDonald's restaurant is at Vinita on the Will Rogers Turnpike. Moscow ranks second in square feet.

- Oklahoma has sent more astronauts into space than any other state.

- The largest stocker feeder cattle market and the largest junior livestock show are at Oklahoma City.

- Oklahoma attracts more tornadoes per square mile than any other area.

- The deepest gas well in the world is located in Oklahoma. It is the 31,441-foot-deep Lone Star No. 1 Bertha Rogers in Washita County.

✔ The world's tallest totem pole is at Foyil.

✔ Oklahoma harvests more mung beans than any other state.

✔ The world's biggest parakeet farm is at Waurika.

✔ Five of the 1988 Miss America contestants had been students at Oklahoma City University (OCU).

✔ Thirty-six of the Oklahoma Miss Teenage America contestants also attended Oklahoma City University.

✔ Oklahoma has sent more baseball players to the major leagues than any other state.

BIBLIOGRAPHY

BOOKS

Blackburn, Bob, *Heart of the Promised Land*, Oklahoma Historical Society, Oklahoma City, 1967.

Blessing, Patrick J., *The British and Irish In Oklahoma*, University of Oklahoma Press, Norman, 1980.

Bryant, Keith L., *Alfalfa Bill Murray*, University of Oklahoma Press, Norman 1968.

Cosby, Hugh E., *History of Moore, Oklahoma*, Cosby Pub., 1977.

Cunningham, *Stillwater Through the Years*, Robert E. Cunningham, Artist Humanities Council of Stillwater, Oklahoma, 1984.

Debo, Angie, *Oklahoma Foot-Loose and Fancy Free*, University of Oklahoma Press, 1949.

Ellsworth, Scott, *Death In A Promised Land, The Tulsa Race Riot of 1921*, Louisiana State University Press, Baton Rouge and London, 1982.

Forbes, Gerald, *Guthrie, Oklahoma's First Capital* University of Oklahoma Press, Norman, 1938.

Franklin, Jimmy Lewis, *Born Sober: Prohibition in Oklahoma, 1907-1959*, University of Oklahoma Press, Norman, 1971.

Faulk, Odie B., *The Making of A Merchant: R. A. Young and T. G. & Y. Stores*, For Oklahoma Heritage Association, by Western Heritage Books, Inc., Oklahoma City, 1980.

Franks, Kenny, *Early Oklahoma Oil, A Photographic History, 1859-1936*, Texas A & M University Press, 1981.

Gibson, Arrell, *Oklahoma: A History of Five Centuries*, University of Oklahoma Press, Norman, 1985.

Graves, Richard S., *Oklahoma Outlaws*, State Printing & Publishing Co., Oklahoma City, 1917.

Green, Donald E., edited by, *Rural Oklahoma*, Oklahoma Historical Society, Oklahoma City, 1977.

Gregory, Jack, and Rennard Strickland, *Sam Houston With the Cherokees, 1829-1833*, University Texas Press, Austin, 1967.

Hickok, Ralph, *Who Was Who In American Sports*, Hawthorn Books, Inc., 1971.

Hinton, Ted, *Ambush, the Real Story of Bonnie and Clyde*, Shoal Creek Publishers, Inc., Austin, Texas, 1976.

Hoig, Stan, *Battle of the Washita*, Doubleday, New York, 1976.

Hoig, Stan, *Oklahoma Land Rush of 1889*, Oklahoma Historical Society, Oklahoma City, 1984.

Hurst, Irvin, *The 46th Star*, Western Heritage Books, Inc., Oklahoma City, 1980.

Jackson, Robert B., *The Remarkable Ride of the Abernathy Boys*, Henry Z. Walck, Inc., New York, 1967.

James, Louise, *Below Devil's Gap*, Perkins Press, Perkins, 1985.

Johnson, Neil, *The Chickasaw Rancher*, Redlands Press, Stillwater, 1960.

Lenburg, Jeff, *The Animated Cartoon Series*, Da Capo Press, New York, 1981.

McCrill, Albert, *And Satan Came Also Came*, Britton Publishing Company, Oklahoma City, 1955.

Mooney, Charles W., *Localized History Pottawatomie County, Oklahoma, to 1907*,Midwest City, 1971, pp. 268-270.

Rohrs, Richard C., *The Germans In Oklahoma*, University of Oklahoma Press, Norman, 1980.

Ruth, Kent and Jim Argo, *Window On The Past, Historic Places In Oklahoma*, Western Heritage Press, Oklahoma City, 1982.

Savage, Jr., William W., *Singing Cowboys and All That Jazz*, University of Oklahoma, Norman, 1983.

Shirley, Glenn, *Pawnee Bill*, University New Mexico Press, 1958.

Steele, Phillip, *The Last Cherokee Warriors*, Pelican Publishing Company, Gretna, 1974.

Stewart, Roy P. and Pendleton Woods, *One of A Kind, the Life of C. R. Anthony*, Oklahoma Heritage Association, Western Heritage Books, Inc., Oklahoma City, 1981.

Teall, Kaye M., *Black History In Oklahoma*, Oklahoma City Public Schools, Oklahoma City, 1971.

Thomas, James H., *The Bunion Derby, Andy Payne and The Great Transcontinental Footrace*, Southwest Heritage Books, Inc., Oklahoma City, 1981.

Wallace, Michael, *Oilman!*, Doubleday, New York, 1988.

Weeks, Jim, *The Sooners, A Story of Oklahoma Football*, The Strode Publishers, Huntsville, Alabama, 1974.

Wise, Lu Celia Wise, *Oklahoma's Blending of Many Cultures*, Pride In Heritage Illustrated Books, 1976.

Womack, John, *The Annals of Cleveland County, Oklahoma 1889-1959, from the Norman Transcript*, Norman, 1981.

Womack, John, *Norman: An Early History, 1820-1900*, Womack, Norman, 1976.

The WPA Guide To 1930s Oklahoma, University of Kansas Press, 1986, compiled by the Writers' Program of the Work Projects Administration In the State of Oklahoma, and Introduction by Anne Hodges Morgan.

Wright, Muriel H., George H. Shirk, and Kenny A. Franks, *Mark of Heritage*, Oklahoma Historical Society, Oklahoma City, 1976.

NEWSPAPERS

Capper's Weekly, October 13, 1987, "Hometown Heartbeat."

The Daily Oklahoman, April 6, 1937; May 30, 1975; May 11, 1971, "Her Birth Beats City's"; August 16, 1974, p. 1, "Xerox Coming 'Home,' Where Process Began"; June 27, 1982; February 2, 1985, "Voice of Donald Duck Dies"; November 18, 1986; June 13, 1988, p. 1, "Western Author Louis L'Amour Dies of Lung Cancer"; July, 1988, p. 1, "DeBarr Scratched From OU Building"; November 18, 1986, "Holes Needed To Probe Lake's Disappearance"; June 13, 1988.

Guthrie State Capital, "A Lady Marshal," March 11, 1893.

New York Times, September 23, 1983, "Publishing: Congress Honors Louis L'Amour."

The Norman Transcript, March 17, 1893, "A Noble Little Lady"; May 2, 1988, p. 10, "Navigation of Arkansas River Adventure In 1935" September 13, 1985; May 8, 1988, July 31, 1988, p. 1, "DeBarr Name To Be Taken Off OU Chemistry Building"; July 20, 1988, "It Could Get Hotter."

The Oklahoma Times Journal, December 23, 1893, "Plucky Miss Curnutt."

The Sunday Oklahoman, June 27, 1982, p. 4, Section A, "Quannah Parker's Descendants Gather At Reunion."

Wichita Beacon Sunday Magazine, August 3, 1924.

MAGAZINES

Chronicles of Oklahoma, Oklahoma Historical Society, 1909 to present.

Oklahoma Today, 1959 to present.

Orbit Magazine, 1963 to 1978.

Reader's Digest, November 1970, p. 121.

INTERVIEWS

William Karty, Moore, Oklahoma, June 23, 1988.

Carol King, Waynoka, Oklahoma, August 1, 1988.

Doyle McCoy, Oklahoma City, July 1988.

Pat McDowell, Oklahoma State Forestry, Oklahoma City, July 1988.

FILMS

"Red Carpet Country," Susan Scull Mathis, Norman Cable TV, 1986.

PHAMPLETS

Oklahoma Department of Tourism, various.

TYPESCRIPT

Oklahoma Department of Commerce.

INDEX

GIVE A BOOK TO A FRIEND

Moments In Oklahoma History, A Book of Trivia. Told in short, often humorous anecdotes, 115 ppg. ISBN 0-9619639-0-5, ppr, $9.95.

Portrait of a Lawman, U.S. Deputy Marshal Heck Thomas. Biography of one of Indian and Oklahoma Territories most famous lawmen. By Bonnie Speer, 172 ppg, ills, index, bibliography. ISBN 0-9619639-3-X, ppr, $11.95.

The Art of Self-Publishing, A Successful Solution to Your Book Publishing Needs. All you need to know to publish, promote and market your own book. By Bonnie Speer, 105 pages, ills. ISBN 1889683-00-0, $10.95.

Write Your Life Story, A Quick Guide for Doing It Yourself from Start to Finish. Ills., 35 ppg, by Bonnie Speer. $5.95.

Hillback To Boggy, by Jess and Bonnie Speer. Destitute Oklahoma family struggles for survival in a tent in the hills during the Great Depression. Ills., ISBN 0-9619639-0-5, ppr. $11.95; 0-9619639-7-2, hrd,$19.95.

Sons of Thunder, by Jess and Bonnie Speer. Sequel to award winning **Hillback To Boggy.** Tag seeks an education. His quest takes him to the war in the South Pacific in 1943 and back again. ISBN 9619639-8-0, ppr, $10.95, ills, 221 pages.

The Great Abraham Lincoln Hijack, 1876 attempt to steal the president's body. Ills., endnotes, index, 214 ppg, by Bonnie Speer. ISBN 9619639-2-1, ppr; $13.95.

Cleveland County, Pride of the Promised Land, a coffee table size, ills, Oklahoma history, 188 ppg. ISBN 0-9430870-2-3, $29.95, hrd.

Send orders to: **RELIANCE PRESS**, 1400 Melrose Drive, Norman, OK 73069. Enclose $2.00 for postage and handling for the first book and 50 cents for each additional book. Oklahoma residents add 7.5% sales tax.